TOP **10**
ORLANDO

W0113936

CONTENTS

4

Introducing Orlando

Welcome to Orlando   6
The Story of Orlando   8
Top 10 Experiences   12
Itineraries   14

18

Top 10 Highlights

Explore the Highlights   20
Magic Kingdom® Park   22
EPCOT®   26
Disney's Hollywood
   Studios®   30
Disney's Animal
   Kingdom® Park   32
Universal Studios
   Florida™   34
Universal's Islands
   of Adventure™   38
The Wizarding World
   of Harry Potter™   42
LEGOLAND®   44
Merritt Island   48
Kennedy Space Center
   Visitor Complex   52

56

Top 10 of Everything

Museums	58
Cultural Venues	60
Thrill Rides	62
Smaller Attractions	64
Parks and Preserves	66
Places to Cool Off	70
Spas	72
Sports and Outdoor Activities	74
Golf Courses	76
Off the Beaten Path	78
Live Music Venues	80
Favorite LGBTQ+ Spots	82
Dining Experiences	84
Places to Shop	86
Orlando for Free	88
Festivals and Events	90
Day Trips South and West	92
Day Trips North and East	94

96

Area by Area

Walt Disney World® Resort and Lake Buena Vista	98
International Drive Area	108
Kissimmee and Beyond	116
Downtown Orlando	122
Winter Park, Maitland, and Eatonville	130

136

Streetsmart

Getting Around	138	Places to Stay	148
Practical Information	142	Index	152
Theme Park Tips	146	Acknowledgments	158

ORLANDO

INTRODUCING

Welcome to Orlando 6

The Story of Orlando 8

Top 10 Experiences 12

Itineraries 14

Chinese pagoda in Lake Eola Park

WELCOME TO
ORLANDO

There's nowhere like Orlando. Famed for its theme parks, the city has become a byword for dream vacations and family fun. Yet while millions flock here to ride the roller coasters, there's more to the city than meets the eye. With Top 10 Orlando, you'll enjoy the best it has to offer.

Ever since Walt Disney opened his ambitious Disney World® Resort here in 1971, Orlando has been a haven for thrill-seekers and families alike. Today, this tourist ecosystem hosts five of the world's busiest theme parks, with attractions from the largest entertainment companies in the world – and more joining the roster every year. Magic Kingdom® Park is jam-packed with beloved rides, Universal Studios Florida™ brings favorite films and TV shows to life, and LEGOLAND® immerses visitors in a nostalgic brick-built world. Numerous park offshoots

also draw the crowds. Venture on a safari at Disney's Animal Kingdom® Park or escape the goblin-guarded Gringotts™ at Universal's Wizarding World of Harry Potter™. Packed with enough adrenaline-inducing rides and family-friendly attractions to fill a bucket-list, this city really is a place where dreams come true.

Exploring beyond the roller coasters also brings its own rewards. An array of lush green spaces, top golf courses, and local wildlife areas provide the perfect place to decompress after a day of theme park fun. The vast Merritt Island, for example, is the second-largest wildlife reserve in Florida. Culture also abounds:

Orlando Museum of Art is packed with striking works of American art while the city's food scene offers Michelin-starred restaurants aplenty. And then there's the unmissable Kennedy Space Center. Here, budding astronauts can see spectacular spacecraft and enjoy state-of-the-art simulations – if you're lucky enough, you might even catch a real rocket launch.

So where to start? With Top 10 Orlando, of course. This pocket-sized guide gets to the heart of the city with simple lists of 10, expert local knowledge, and comprehensive maps, helping you turn an ordinary trip into an extraordinary one.

THE STORY OF
ORLANDO

Orlando changed dramatically with the arrival of Walt Disney World®
in 1971, but behind the city's modern veneer lies a rich past. Once home
to Indigenous peoples, Orlando was passed between various colonizers
before being ceded to the US. Here's the story of how it came to be.

Europeans Arrive

Central Florida has been inhabited for thousands of years. Archaeological remains in the area suggest that Indigenous communities – including the Ais, Apalachee, Calusa, Timucua, and Tocobaga – were living here some 12,000 years before European settlers arrived. The Timucua were the largest group in the area, with historians estimating their numbers at around 50,000 members in the early 16th century. Everything would change, however, with the arrival of Europeans.

After plundering resources along the American Atlantic coast, Spanish explorer and conquistador Ponce de Leon arrived on the southern coast of Florida in 1513, naming the region La Florida (the place of flowers). Over the next 25 years, Spanish ships brought hundreds of settlers to the region, who caused irrevocable damage to Indigenous groups. Communities were forcibly displaced, and new infectious diseases and brutal warfare decimated populations; the Napituca Massacre of Timucua people in 1539 was the first large-scale massacre by Europeans on American soil.

A Period of Conflict

As centuries passed, conflict ruled the region. The French and British staked their claims on Florida at various times throughout the 17th and 18th centuries, though ultimately the Spanish retained control. Violent clashes also occurred between what were now United States forces and Seminole groups (Indigenous peoples who settled in Florida in the 1700s). In 1816,

Timucua Indigenous peoples looking for gold

General Andrew Jackson with members of his troop

General Andrew Jackson attacked the Seminoles, who harbored people who had escaped from slavery; the war that developed led to Florida becoming part of the US in 1821. In 1823, the Treaty of Moultrie Creek forced the Seminoles into a reservation, which encompassed the area of Orlando. As American settlement in Central Florida increased, the US government passed the Indian Removal Act in 1830, which aimed to forcibly move all Indigenous peoples west of the Mississippi River. The resulting conflicts developed into the brutal Second and Third Seminole Wars.

Orlando Becomes Official

Originally known to Europeans as Jernigan (after the first European to permanently settle there), Orlando had remained a relatively rural part of Florida until the Seminole Wars. During the Second War, the Americans created a fortified settlement at Fort Gatlin (just south of the city limits); by 1840, a small community had grown up around the fort. The town that would become today's city was established, with early infrastructure laid out in 1857.

It wasn't long after Orlando was founded that it entered its so-called Golden Era. Plantations, orchards, and cattle ranches sprang up as a result of the area's sunny climate and suitable terrain. In the latter part of the 19th century, Orlando became the hub of the state's citrus industry.

Moments in History

Pre 1513
Indigenous peoples, including the Ais, Apalachee, Calusa, Timucua, and Tocobaga, populate Central Florida.

1513
Ponce de Leon is the first European to explore Florida, arriving on the southern coast and naming the region La Florida.

1763
Conflict between colonizing nations recedes as Britain, France, and Spain bring an end to the Seven Years' War (also known as the French and Indian War).

1783
The American Revolutionary War ends. Britain relinquishes territories east of the Mississippi River, including Florida.

1816–1858
The Seminole Wars see Indigenous groups sustain heavy losses. Only around 100 Seminoles survive the Third War.

1861
Florida becomes the third state to secede from the Union, behind Mississippi and South Carolina.

1885
Orlando is officially incorporated as a city; the 1890 Florida census lists its population at around 3,000 people.

1930
The city opens its first airport and its population reaches around 30,000.

1971
After years of construction, and at a cost of $400 million, Walt Disney World® opens its gates. Throughout the 1980s and 90s, a flurry of theme parks follow, including EPCOT® and Disney's Animal Kingdom®.

2021
The Kennedy Space Center Visitor Complex opens Planet Play, an immersive, multistory play area for children.

Changing Demographics

Enjoying unprecedented boom times among the orange groves, the town of Orlando was incorporated with 85 official residents in 1875. Just ten years later, Orlando officially became a city, with the 1890 Florida census listing a population of just under 3,000 people. Yet the good times didn't last forever. As a result of an unexpected harsh freeze in the winter of 1894, many independent farmers lost their livelihoods, and large produce conglomerates bought the vacated land. After a short period of decline, Orlando regained its status, with huge investments in statewide infrastructure, including the first passenger flights, giving the city a boost. Numerous families moved back to support the opening of the city's landmark entertainment center, The Grand Theater, and by 1930, Orlando had its first airport. Its population soon skyrocketed to 30,000.

A new period of prosperity had arrived and, bolstered by its warm and sunny climate, Orlando began its pivot to hospitality in the 1920s.

Walt Disney, founder of the Disney theme parks

A parade taking place at Universal Studios Florida™

Dreams Come True

The most significant moment in Orlando's history came in the 1960s, when American entrepreneur and animator Walt Disney bought swaths of land in Florida. His Californian theme park Disneyland® had opened to acclaim in 1955, and on November 15, 1965, "Uncle" Walt announced that Orlando would be the location for an even more ambitious project. The news triggered an immediate land rush, with hotels and hospitality brands buying up any available swampland, often for millions of dollars. At around the same time, NASA established Merritt Island (and what would become the Kennedy Space Center) as a launch site for hundreds of space flight missions. Orlando was the place to be.

In 1971, at a cost of $400 million, Walt Disney World® opened its gates, and Mickey Mouse escorted the first visitors into the Magic Kingdom®. In the first two years, the theme park sold 20 million tickets and employed 13,000 people, making Orlando the fastest-growing city in the state. Plenty of businesses sought to capitalize on this success, with a deluge of companies moving operations to the area and a slew of theme parks opening their

doors: EPCOT® opened in 1982, Disney's Hollywood Studios® in 1989, and Disney's Animal Kingdom® Park in 1998. Over the course of just 30 years, something akin to a modern-day gold rush had taken place – and Orlando's foreseeable future was assured.

Orlando Today

Today, Orlando spearheads America's hospitality industry, attracting over 70 million people every year. Disney and Universal continue to unveil new rides and attractions, many driven by successful movie franchises. The city seems set on continual expansion, fueled by dependably huge revenue streams – and a hint of Uncle Walt's spirit of imagination.

This success attracts trouble, however. State governors have brought in increasingly dogmatic policies, with 2019 appointee Ron DeSantis publicly at loggerheads with the Disney corporation over its self-governing status. Orlando has also witnessed dark times amid its sunny spells, with the 2016 attack on an LGBTQ+ nightclub devastating the city. For now, though, Orlando's theme parks remain islands of escapism, never failing to deliver on their promise of a dream vacation.

TOP 10
EXPERIENCES

Planning a trip to Orlando? Whether you're visiting for the first time or making a return trip, there are some things you simply shouldn't miss out on. To make the most of your time here – and to maximize your enjoyment of the theme parks and beyond – be sure to add these experiences to your list.

1 Take superstar selfies
Want to meet your favorite cartoon characters? Elaborately costumed actors can be found in Orlando's best theme parks, and they're always up for a selfie. Catch them at parades, special events, and around any rides they're associated with for a spontaneous "celebrity" photo opportunity.

2 Escape to space
It's not every day you get to explore real-life rockets. Jet over to Kennedy Space Center (p52) to see dozens of spectacular spacecraft and artifacts that have returned from outer space missions. You can test your astronaut abilities in a Space Shuttle launch simulation, too.

3 See the world in a day
Celebrate Oktoberfest, gaze upon the Eiffel Tower, unwind in Japanese gardens: EPCOT® (p26) takes visitors on a journey around the world. Part of this theme park, the World Showcase, features 11 pavilions from different countries across the globe, presenting their incredible landmarks and customs.

4 Chill out in cool corners
Need a break from that dazzling Florida sun? Orlando has you covered. Featuring a great choice of fun-filled water parks, this city knows how to cool down. It's also a short drive to the sea where famous sandy stretches, like Cocoa Beach (p94) and Daytona Beach (p94), await.

5 Get your culture fix

Don't overlook Downtown Orlando. The city most famous for its theme parks is also home to some of Florida's best cultural institutions. The Orlando Museum of Art *(p123)* is a flagship museum while the Orlando Science Center *(p123)* offers family fun.

6 Step into Hogwarts

The world of the *Harry Potter* books has become a global phenomenon and nowhere is it better brought to life than in The Wizarding World of Harry Potter™ *(p42)*. Within this magical park, fans can ride the Hogwarts™ Express or swish and flick their own wands.

7 Spot local wildlife

Florida's climate means that the state is home to over 500 species of bird and 4,000 animal species, making it the seventh-most biodiverse state in the nation. Head to the vast reserves like Merritt Island *(p48)* to appreciate some of this incredible wildlife.

8 Enjoy high-end dining

From lovely local farmers' markets in Winter Park *(p131)* to exclusive theme-park restaurants, Orlando has a surprisingly dynamic and varied food scene. Long-time favorites include THE BOATHOUSE® *(p104)* and Victoria & Albert's *(p104)*.

9 Ride a world-class roller coaster

With dozens of high-speed rides and roller coasters, this city is perfect for adrenaline lovers. Flagship coasters such as Revenge of the Mummy® at Universal Studios Florida™ *(p34)* are sure to have fans screaming for more.

10 Find some peace

Orlando can invite sensory overload, so it's important to find time away from the theme parks. Ascend above the clamor in a tethered helium-filled balloon, walk a nature trail in a national park, or unwind in a luxurious spa. You'll feel all the better for it.

ITINERARIES

Visiting your dream theme park, exploring the Kennedy Space Center, wandering around Downtown: there's a lot to see and do in this city. With places to drink, or take in the view, these itineraries offer ways to spend 2 days and 4 days in Orlando.

2 DAYS

Day 1

Morning
On your first day, rise early to visit the place that started it all: Disney's Magic Kingdom® Park (p22). Aim to arrive half an hour before the park's official opening time (or stay on site if you really want to beat the crowds). Once in, it's time to tick off some of the classic rides while the lines are still short: the Jungle Cruise and Big Thunder Mountain Railroad make for a thrilling start to the day. Mornings are

> **SHOP**
> If you're looking for a Harry Potter–themed souvenir, head to Ollivanders™ (p43). At this magical shop the wand chooses the wizard – will yours feature unicorn hair or phoenix feathers?

also a good time for meet-and-greets, so keep an eye out for your favorite characters as you explore. Need to refuel? Lunch at Liberty Tree Tavern or Skipper Canteen within the park (book ahead).

Afternoon
Ease yourself into the afternoon with a whimsical boat ride at It's a Small World, a beloved attraction with an undeniably catchy theme tune. Generations of Disney fans also enjoy the nearby Haunted Mansion®, another slow-moving ride with a hint of horror. Want a change of pace? Seek out the park's high-tech TRON Lightcycle/Run, a flashy coaster in the Tomorrowland area, followed by swashbuckling fun at the Pirates of the Caribbean® boat cruise. For dinner, a magical meal awaits at Cinderella's Royal Table (book well in advance for this one).

Disney's Magic Kingdom® Park

Voodoo Doughnut at Universal CityWalk™

Day 2

Morning

On your second day, head to the Universal Orlando Resort™ where various parks offer something for everyone. Adrenaline-lovers should make for Universal's Islands of Adventure™ (p38), where a host of thrilling rides are sure to keep you screaming. As with all theme parks, arrive before the gates open to hit up popular coasters (the Incredible Hulk Coaster®, Amazing Adventures of Spider-Man®, and Skull Island Reign of Kong are favorites). For Potterheads and fantasy fans, the neighboring Wizarding World of Harry Potter™ (p42) will be top of the list. Ample adventures are on offer here: ride the Hogwarts™ Express or face your fear of Dementors on Harry Potter and the Forbidden Journey™.

Afternoon

Take a late lunch at the Leaky Cauldron before heading to explore Universal Studios Florida™ (p34). Each of the park's eight themed areas are situated around a huge lagoon, promising an exciting combination of rides, shows, and attractions. Younger kids will love the Despicable Me Minion Mayhem and The Simpsons Ride™, while big kids and adults are spoiled for choice. Seek out the action-packed Transformers: The Ride-3D, speedy Fast & Furious: Supercharged™ and spooky Revenge of the Mummy®. Wind down after a busy day with dinner at one of the restaurants in CityWalk™ (p87).

> **VIEW**
> It's virtually compulsory to take a photograph in front of the dreamy Cinderella Castle at the Magic Kingdom® Park. If you can time it with a Disney character meet-and-greet, then all the better.

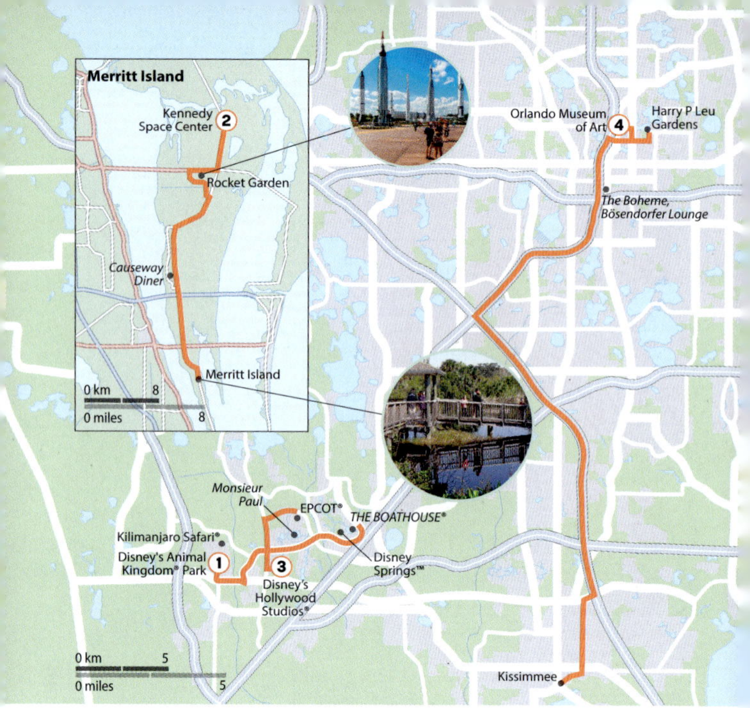

Merritt Island

Kennedy Space Center ②

Rocket Garden

Causeway Diner

Merritt Island

0 km   8
0 miles   8

Orlando Museum of Art ④   Harry P Leu Gardens

The Boheme, Bösendorfer Lounge

Monsieur Paul

EPCOT®   *THE BOATHOUSE®*

Kilimanjaro Safari®

Disney's Animal Kingdom® Park ①   ③   Disney Springs™

Disney's Hollywood Studios®

0 km   5
0 miles   5

Kissimmee

4 DAYS

Day 1

Be sure to have a big breakfast on your first day in Orlando: you're visiting the world's largest theme park. Dedicated to animal conservation, Disney's Animal Kingdom® Park *(p32)* is home to 300 species of animals and birds, as well as countless roller coasters. To start your adventure, spot roaming hyenas and hulking elephants on the guided Kilimanjaro Safari® (it's less busy in the morning). Next, it's time to hit the rides. Fly over Pandora's other-worldly landscape on Avatar Flight of Passage or speed past prehistoric reptiles on DINOSAUR. Places such as Yak & Yeti Restaurant or Restauranto-saurus are perfect for a lunch pit stop. Once you've had your fill of this animal-obsessed park, decamp to Disney Springs™ *(p99)*. This entertainment district is packed with shops and restaurants – THE BOATHOUSE® is a go-to for dinner.

Illuminated landscapes in Avatar Flight of Passage

Day 2

After a busy theme park day, it's time for a change of scenery. Just east of Orlando is the spectacular Kennedy Space Center *(p52)*, a treasure trove of rockets and space-themed artifacts. It makes sense to explore it in chrono-logical order, gazing at the Mercury and Gemini spacecraft before covering the

🍵 **DRINK**
Orlando's nightlife scene is lively and inclusive, with much of the action concentrated around Wall Street Plaza *(p127)*. This neon-lit area is packed with bars, clubs, and late-night restaurants.

famous Apollo missions. After lunch at the Rocket Garden café, it's a half-hour drive to Merritt Island *(p48)*. This vast National Wildlife Refuge is home to 330 birds and over 30 mammal species, many of which are endangered or rare. Keep an eye out for the state's cutest sea mammal, the manatee. On your way out, stop for dinner at one of the low-key restaurants on the Causeway.

Day 3

It's back to the theme parks today, with an early arrival at Disney's Hollywood Studios® *(p30)*. This beloved park is dedicated to celebrating the worlds of film, TV, music, and theater. Sci-fi fans will want to head straight to Star Wars: Galaxy's Edge®, an area not so far far away, with themed rides and attractions. Younger visitors, meanwhile, might prefer the Muppets-themed attractions around Grand Avenue. For lunch, fill your boots with American comfort food at the kitsch 50's Prime Time Café *(p105)*. Next up it's EPCOT® *(p26)*, an iconic theme park famous for its World Showcase Pavilions. Before you venture around the world, however, tick off some of the rides. The slower Spaceship Earth will ease you in before you ride the reverse-launch Guardians of the Galaxy: Cosmic Rewind. As evening approaches, amble around the World Showcase, ending in France where you can treat yourself to French cuisine at Monsieur Paul.

Day 4

On your final day in Orlando, take some time to explore the city itself. Start at the Orlando Museum of Art *(p123)*,

which houses incredible American art – with special exhibitions changing monthly. Next, find some serenity at the beautifully landscaped Harry P. Leu Gardens (a-half hour walk away), where butterflies flutter beneath shady oak trees. There are plenty of places to stop for lunch around here. To top off your day, drive over to Kissimmee to spot some gators – high-speed, 90-minute swamp tours *(p120)* race around the area, giving visitors glimpses of these snappy reptiles. As evening approaches, head back to Orlando for fresh seafood at The Boheme *(p127)* restaurant. And, if your flight isn't too early the next day, farewell drinks at the Bösendorfer Lounge *(p126)*.

🚌 **TRANSPORTATION**
Visitors can explore Merritt Island by car or boat. The latter is the best way to get up-close to wildlife but driving can be just as rewarding – take the Black Point Wildlife Drive for fantastic views of the area.

Exploring the lush nature reserves of Kissimmee

TOP 10 HIGHLIGHTS

Explore the Highlights	20
Magic Kingdom® Park	22
EPCOT®	26
Disney's Hollywood Studios®	30
Disney's Animal Kingdom® Park	32
Universal Studios Florida™	34
Universal's Islands of Adventure™	38
The Wizarding World of Harry Potter™	42
LEGOLAND®	44
Merritt Island	48
Kennedy Space Center Visitor Complex	52

Rocket at Kennedy Space Center Visitor Complex

EXPLORE THE
HIGHLIGHTS

There are some sights in Orlando you simply shouldn't miss, and it's these attractions that make the Top 10. Discover what makes each one a must-see on the following pages.

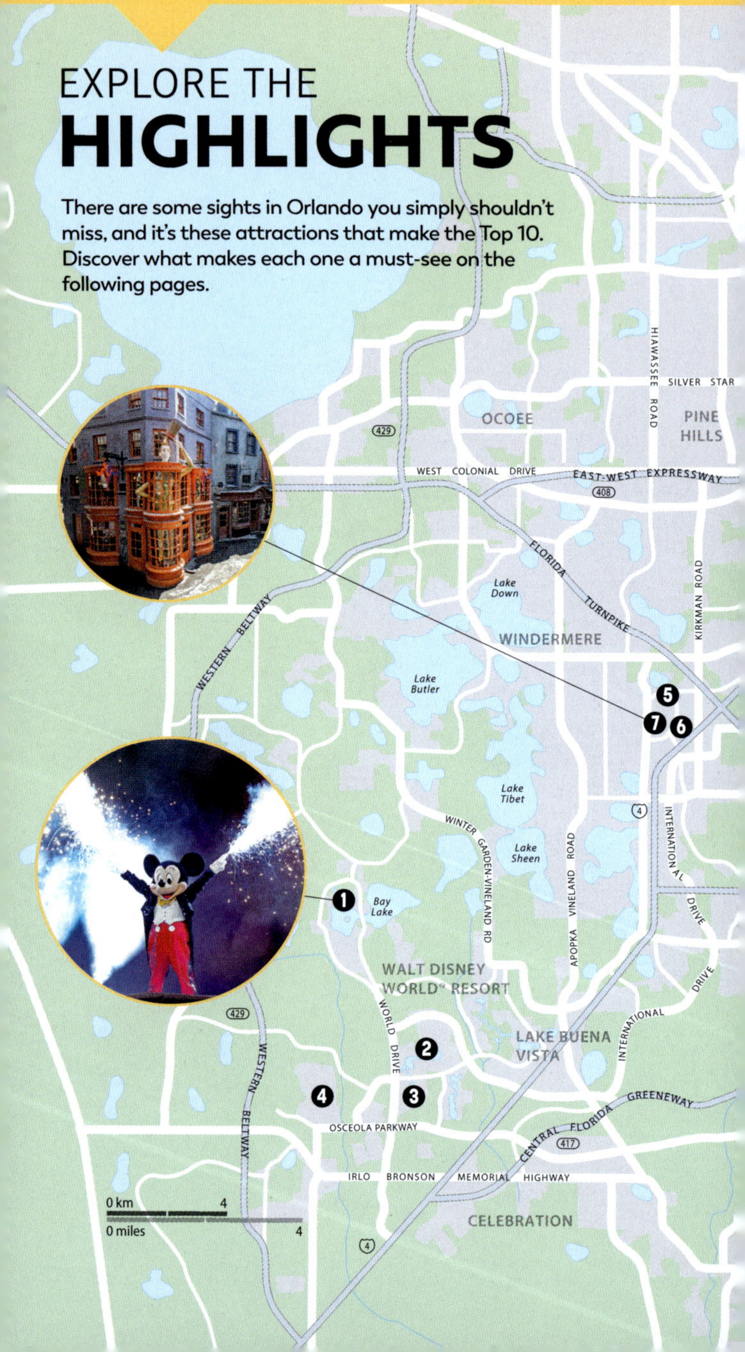

Area of main map

Apopka

ORLANDO

Walt Disney World® Resort

St Cloud

Cocoa

Haines City

Winter Haven

Lake Wales

Melbourne

0 km 30

0 miles 30

ORANGE BLOSSOM TRAIL

ROAD

MILLS AVENUE

EAST COLONIAL DRIVE

DOWNTOWN

EAST-WEST EXPRESSWAY

CENTRAL FLORIDA GREENEWAY

ORANGE AVENUE

JOHN YOUNG PARKWAY

OAK RIDGE ROAD

SKY LAKE

PINE CASTLE

SAND LAKE ROAD

BEACHLINE EXPRESSWAY

TAFT

FLORIDA TURNPIKE

ORANGE BLOSSOM TRAIL

JOHN

YOUNG PARKWAY

KISSIMMEE

❶ Magic Kingdom® Park

❷ EPCOT®

❸ Disney's Hollywood Studios®

❹ Disney's Animal Kingdom® Park

❺ Universal Studios Florida™

❻ Universal's Islands of Adventure™

❼ The Wizarding World of Harry Potter™

❽ LEGOLAND®

❾ Merritt Island

❿ Kennedy Space Center Visitor Complex

MAGIC KINGDOM® PARK

🅿 V1 🏠 World Drive 🕐 9am–10pm Mon–Fri, 9am–11pm Sat & Sun
🅦 disneyworld.com ⬈

The park that started Disney's vast Florida empire in 1971, Magic Kingdom® hosts an incredible collection of more than 40 major attractions and countless smaller ones. It has long been the area's most popular theme park, featuring six captivating lands and welcoming millions of guests every year.

1 Pirates of the Caribbean®

Timbers are a-shiver as your boat cruises past a town under siege from a band of rum-soaked, Audio-Animatronic® buccaneers. With dank dungeons and yo-ho-hos, you'll experience all scurvy pirate life here.

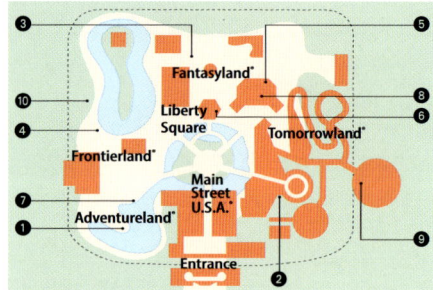

Magic Kingdom® Park Site Plan

2 Buzz Lightyear's Space Ranger Spin

Use the laser cannons on the dashboard to set off sight-and-sound effects as you hurtle through the sky and help *Toy Story*'s famous hero save the world.

3 Peter Pan's Flight

Begin your journey from the nursery where Michael, Wendy, and John sleep. A flying pirate galleon then soars over the nighttime sights of London and arrives in Never Land, where Peter Pan battles Captain Hook to save Wendy and her brothers.

4 Tiana's Bayou Adventure

Opened in 2024, this boat ride through the waters in Frontierland® is inspired by the 2009 film *The Princess and the Frog*. It takes visitors on a wonderful musical adventure through Louisiana.

5 Seven Dwarfs Mine Train

Ideal for visitors who aren't keen on the park's

> **TOP TIP**
>
> Most rides at Magic Kingdom® have a minimum height of 40 inches (102 cm).

Goofy in front of the Cinderella Castle

A canopied tramp steamer on the Jungle Cruise

PARK GUIDE It takes more than 20 minutes to get from the parking lots (via tram, boat, or monorail) to the Magic Kingdom® entrance. Once inside, pick up a map and times guide. Access real-time info on your smartphone with the My Disney Experience app. You'll need at least a day, preferably two, to fully explore the park.

more intense rides, this twisty coaster trundles through the Enchanted Forest and diamond mines.

6 Prince Charming Regal Carrousel

This restored 1917 carousel has handsome wooden horses and an organ that plays Disney classics. A guaranteed hit, no matter your age.

7 The Jungle Cruise

Cruise through the African Congo, Amazon rainforest, and along the Egyptian Nile, where animatronic animals roam free. The real appeal of this classic ride is the captain's corny commentary.

8 The Many Adventures of Winnie the Pooh

Pooh, Eeyore, and a host of A. A. Milne's lovable characters come to life in this tranquil ride through the Hundred Acre Wood.

9 Space Mountain®

Orlando's first in-the-dark roller coaster is a rocket ride through hairpin turns and drops at what feels like breakneck speed. Galactic details and sound effects enhance this classic thrill ride.

10 Big Thunder Mountain Railroad

Not the fastest coaster, but the turns and dips, and realistic scenery, combine to make this an exciting trip on a runaway mine train through gold-rush country.

The Big Thunder Mountain Railroad ride

Shows and Next-Best Rides

1. Tomorrowland® Transit Authority PeopleMover

High above the ground, this informative 10-minute narrated tour of Tomorrowland® offers some of the loveliest views in the park (especially after dark), and a well-earned opportunity to relax after a great deal of walking. Board the PeopleMover near the Astro Orbiter for a journey through Space Mountain and a peek inside several other attractions along the way.

2. Disney Enchantment

This dazzling multimedia show lights up the sky above Cinderella Castle on numerous nights throughout the year (sometimes twice a night in the summer months and school holidays). The castle itself comes to life with a stunning projection show, all set to a moving musical score. The projection can best be seen from Main Street U.S.A.®, as well as anywhere on the front side of the castle.

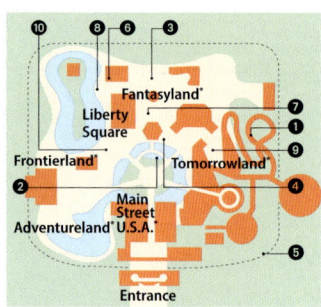

Magic Kingdom® Park Site Plan

3. Under the Sea – Journey of the Little Mermaid

Embark on an enchanting musical adventure with this ride, which takes you below the waves without getting wet. The ride re-creates iconic scenes from the Disney classic with the help of animatronics and video. Afterward, make sure to visit Ariel's Grotto and spend some time with everyone's favorite mermaid.

4. Cinderella Castle

The must-see stop on any tour of the Magic Kingdom® is the Cinderella Castle. Standing 185 ft (56 m) high, this park icon is a sight to behold. Complete with Gothic spires, it's the quintessential fairy-tale castle, reminiscent of Neuschwanstein, Germany's famed castle. Inside is Cinderella's Royal Table (p105), the most sought-after dining experience in Walt Disney World®.

5. Walt Disney World® Railroad

The antique steam-driven trains that travel this 2-km- (1.5-mile-) perimeter track offer a good overview of the park's sights, but more importantly allow you to get around without the legwork. The 20-minute ride stops at Walt Disney World® Railroad Station, Main Street U.S.A.®, Frontierland®, and magical Fantasyland®.

6. Haunted Mansion®

Ghosts come out to socialize on this slow-moving spooky favorite, which sits at the end of Liberty Square. Passengers board "Doom Buggies" and take a ride through dark and dusty rooms in a haunted house full of thrills. More amusing than scary (for all but younger children), it's a cult classic, and one of the most popular rides in the park.

7. Mickey's PhilharMagic

Disney magic meets Disney music in a 3D movie spectacular starring Mickey Mouse, Donald Duck, and other favorite Disney characters animated in a way never seen before. It is located in the PhilharMagic concert hall in Fantasyland®.

8. It's a Small World

Small kids and nostalgic adults alike adore this slow cruise around the world, where colorfully costumed

Ariel's Grotto, Under the Sea – Journey of the Little Mermaid

Cruising through the wonderfully kitschy It's a Small World ride

characters portray the world's cultures. There's just no avoiding it: the catchy theme tune will stick in your head for months.

9. Mad Tea Party

Round and round you go, spinning in whimsically painted pastel-colored teacups on spinning platforms. Riders control how much their own teacups spin on this usually tame ride, but if you get dizzy easily, this may not be for you.

10. Hall of Presidents

Every U.S. president is represented by fluid Audio-Animatronics® in this fascinating educational show that highlights the wizardry of Walt Disney Imagineers.

EPCOT®

W2 🏠 EPCOT Center Dr, Walt Disney World® Resort 🕐 Future World: 9am–9:30pm daily; World Showcase: 11am–9pm daily, with extended seasonal hours 🌐 disneyworld.com 🔗

EPCOT®, or the Experimental Prototype Community of Tomorrow, was designed as a town where people could live and work in technological splendor. After Walt Disney's death in 1966, the idea change dramatically and in 1982 it opened as a thrilling theme park, with people of all ages thronging its premises everyday.

1 Test Track
After designing and digitally road testing your own concept car, hop on a SIM Car for a driving adventure that takes you flying along straightaways and steep curves, reaching speeds of 65 mph (104 km/h). You must be at least 40 inches (102 cm) tall.

2 Mission: SPACE®
This popular thrill ride takes you on a high-intensity journey into space with a crash landing on Mars. There are two versions to choose from, depending on how prone to motion sickness you are.

3 Journey into Imagination with Figment
An open house at Dr. Channing's Imagination Institute is turned inside out by Figment, a playful purple dragon. Figment causes chaos as the tour visits five sensory-themed labs, before moving to the dragon's own upside-down home.

4 The Seas with Nemo & Friends
Board a "clamobile" and join an undersea adventure with some familiar friends to help find Nemo. Also in this pavilion are Turtle Talk with Crush and Sea Base Alpha.

5 Turtle Talk with Crush
Kids can ask Crush questions during this

> **EAT**
> Epcot®'s World Showcase restaurants have great food. Try to book well in advance.

Enjoying the high-speed Test Track ride

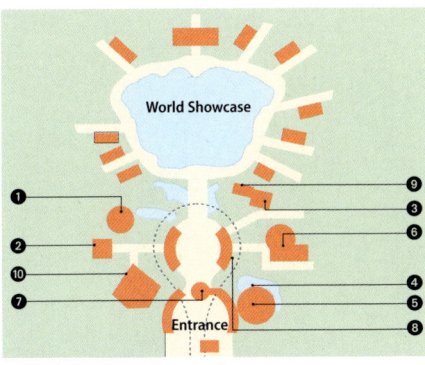

EPCOT® (Future World) Site Plan

unscripted, digitally animated 10-minute show. Characters from both *Finding Nemo* and *Finding Dory* are featured here.

6 Soarin' Around the World

Feel the exhilarating rush of this free-flying hang-gliding adventure over several magnificent landscapes around the globe. You must be 40 inches (102 cm) tall.

7 Spaceship Earth

The ride inside isn't the most exciting, but this gigantic geosphere, symbol of EPCOT®, is an engineering marvel. Its 11,324 aluminum panels absorb the rain rather than letting it run off.

8 Living with the Land

Go on a 13-minute boat ride through three diverse environments – rainforest, desert, and prairie. The ride is then followed by a look at agricultural experiments, including hydroponics and gardening in simulated Martian soil.

9 Disney & Pixar Short Film Festival

Put on a pair of special glasses and experience three brilliant short films in 4D. The festival lasts for around 18 minutes, after which you can discover the creative journey behind the stories through captivating displays outside the theater.

10 Guardians of the Galaxy: Cosmic Rewind

Disney's first ever reverse-launch ride, this is also one of the world's largest enclosed roller coasters. A 360-degree rotation allows riders to truly enjoy the planetarium-like exhibits.

PARK GUIDE

Just beyond the main entrance is Spaceship Earth (Future World area). The World Showcase Lagoon and the 11 nations (p28) are farther away, with handy boat shuttles available to the Germany and Morocco pavilions. A second entrance, at International Gateway, is accessible from Disney's Yacht Club, Beach Club, and BoardWalk Inn resorts.

Spaceship Earth's dazzling LED lighting design

World Showcase Pavilions

**Entrance to EPCOT's®
Mexico pavilion**

1. Mexico
Surrounded by jungle landscaping stands an immense Mayan temple, inside of which mariachi bands play under a perpetually starlit sky. The plaza bustles with artisans peddling their wares. Visit the Mexican countryside aboard the Gran Fiesta Tour, an 8-minute boat ride with an animated element starring Donald Duck.

2. China
The CircleVision movie, Reflections of China, is a fascinating journey through China's natural and artificial riches. The pavilion features a 15th-century Ming dynasty temple, a ceremonial gate, and tranquil gardens. The Yong Feng Shangdian Department Store is a treasure trove of Asian goodies. Try not to miss the dynamic Dragon Legend Acrobats, who perform several times each day.

3. Germany
In this archetypal German village, where Oktoberfest is celebrated year-round, you'll find a miniature model railroad, including a wonderfully detailed Bavarian Village. The Biergarten restaurant (with live brass band music) serves traditional food, and shops sell everything from Hummel figurines to wines.

4. American Adventure
Enhance your knowledge of U.S. history in a 30-minute dramatization featuring Audio-Animatronic® actors. Mark Twain and Benjamin Franklin explain key events such as the writing of the Declaration of Independence, while Susan B. Anthony speaks out for women's rights. The Voices of Liberty singers perform in the main hall of the pavilion, which is modeled on Philadelphia's Liberty Hall.

5. Japan
A breathtaking five-story pagoda, based on Nara's 8th-century Horyuji temple, forms the centerpiece of this architecturally stunning pavilion. The traditional Japanese gardens are also impressive, and great for escaping the crowds. The peace is occasionally broken by the beat of drums – the Matsuriza troupe put on one of the best shows in EPCOT®.

6. Morocco
Look for the Koutoubia minaret, a replica of the tower from a 12th-century mosque in Marrakesh. Inside this pavilion, the typical souk architecture is embellished by beautiful carvings and mosaics. The authentic marketplace is full of hard-to-resist crafts and you can see carpets being woven.

7. Norway
In the cobblestone courtyard of Norway's pavilion, the residents of Arendelle are celebrating the Winter in Summer Festival. Hop

aboard a log for a *Frozen*-themed snowy ride. Akershus Royal Banquet Hall (a replica of Oslo's 14th-century castle) houses a restaurant.

8. France

This beautiful pavilion sports a scale replica of the Eiffel Tower among other sights focused on French art, architecture, and literature. Another highlight is Impressions de France, an 18-minute, five-screen movie that sweeps through glorious land-scapes, accompanied by music by various French composers.

9. United Kingdom

Examples of typical British architecture through the ages line the lovely cobblestone streets here. Many are home to an array of shops selling quintessential British merch-andise (teas, china, and more). Add-ing to the area's charm is a maze that offers exploration and fun for all ages. Additionally, a bandstand situated in the heart of this locale hosts live music performances every day.

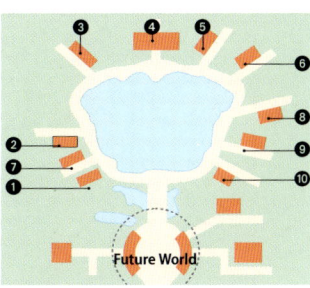

EPCOT® (World Showcase) Site Plan

10. Canada

The star attraction here is the inspirational 360-degree CircleVision movie, Canada Far and Wide, which reveals some of the country's scenic wonders. Outside, Canada's rugged terrain is convincingly re-created. You can explore gardens based on Victoria's Butchart Gardens, a replica of an Indigenous Canadian village, and the Northwest Mercantile store, selling crafts and maple syrup.

Vibrant facade of the Canada pavilion

DISNEY'S HOLLYWOOD STUDIOS®

⬛ W3 🏠 EPCOT® Resorts Blvd 🕐 9am–9pm daily Ⓦ disneyworld.com ✦

From the set-like streetscapes to its lineup of thrilling rides and fantastic stage productions – all based on blockbuster movies and TV shows – Disney's Hollywood Studios® aims to bring the magic of the movies to life. Since its opening in 1989, the park has continued to evolve, combining the nostalgia of Hollywood with the movies of today.

1 Indiana Jones Epic Stunt Spectacular
This action-packed show sees Indiana Jones take on the bad guys with daring stunts, last-minute escapes, and a movie-worthy finale.

2 Toy Story Land
Enjoy the estate of Toy Story where Woody, Jessie, and their friends have fun in Andy's backyard. Popular rides here include Slinky Dog Dash and Alien Swirling Saucers.

3 Star Tours®
Climb in and buckle up: your 40-seat spacecraft is going on a *Star Wars*-inspired, flight-motion simulated 3D journey, riddled with thrilling dips, bumps, and laser fire.

4 Mickey & Minnie's Runaway Railway
Climb aboard an out-of-control train and take a whirlwind ride through the whimsical world of Mickey and Minnie Mouse as they try to save you from disaster.

> 🍴 **EAT**
> Try American classics in a 1950s-style convertible while watching B-movies at the Sci-Fi Dine-In Theater *(p105).*

Mickey & Minnie's Runaway Railway

Colorful rides at Toy Story Land

but by then it's far too late. Your limo zooms from 0 to 60 mph (97 km/h) in 2.8 seconds and into multiple inversions as Aerosmith songs blare at 32,000 watts.

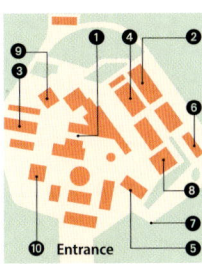

Disney's Hollywood Studios® Site Plan

7 Fantasmic!
Lasers, fireworks, waterborne images, Disney tunes, and a sorcerer mouse are the stars of this end-of-the-day extravaganza *(p103)* that pits the forces of good against Disney villains such as Maleficent and Cruella de Vil. Performance times vary seasonally.

8 Twilight Zone Tower of Terror™
The spooky surroundings are but a facade hiding the real terror, a 13-story fall. Many consider it Disney's best thrill ride.

9 Muppet™ Vision 3D
Miss Piggy, Kermit, and the rest of the crew star in a show celebrating both Jim Henson's legacy and Disney's own legendary special-effects wizardry and Audio-Animatronics®.

10 Jedi Training: Trials of the Temple
Sign up early for this 20-minute training session led by a Jedi Master. It's one of the most sought-after experiences in the park.

PARK GUIDE
Pick up a map from guest services, by the entrance. For real-time information on schedules, wait times, visiting celebrities, and closures, download the My Disney Experience app. The park is less busy at the start of the week, when visitors hit the Magic Kingdom® and EPCOT®, and can be tackled in one day.

5 Beauty and the Beast Live on Stage
The music from the movie is enough to sell this Broadway-style show, but the sets, costumes, and production numbers are spectacular, too.

6 Rock 'n' Roller Coaster® Starring Aerosmith
A sign warns "prepare to merge as you've never merged before,"

Lobby of the Twilight Zone Tower of Terror™

DISNEY'S ANIMAL KINGDOM® PARK

📍 V3 🏠 Savannah Circle 🕐 8am–6pm daily, with extended seasonal hours
🌐 disneyworld.com 📱

As the name implies, wildlife rules at the fourth and largest of Disney's parks, which is home to 300 species of animals and birds spread across 500 acres (2 sq km) of lush landscape. Conservation is at the core here, with visitors observing the animals from a distance.

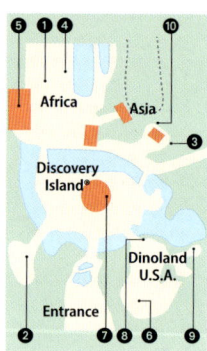

Disney's Animal Kingdom® Park Site Plan

1 Kilimanjaro Safaris®

The park's most popular ride puts visitors on a large safari jeep to bump along dirt tracks through the savanna in search of black rhinos, lions, and zebras. While most active early in the morning, the animals are just as visible during the evening safaris.

2 Pandora – The World of Avatar

Witness floating mountains, trees, and the Valley of Mo'ara during the day, and enjoy the glowing lights at night in this fantasy world. Do not miss the Flight of Passage and Na'Vi River Journey rides.

3 Expedition Everest

In this thrill-filled adventure, your train ascends the snowcapped mountain, before coming to an abrupt stop at a tangled track. You're then

> **TOP TIP**
>
> The animals are most active at opening time and an hour before closing.

Clockwise from right
Expedition Everest's treacherous mountain; lion spotted during the Kilimanjaro Safaris®; DINOSAUR ride at Animal Kingdom®

sent careening backward in complete darkness, twisting and turning through caverns and canyons, with the Yeti lurking in the shadows. You must be 44 inches (112 cm) to ride.

4 Gorilla Falls Exploration Trail®

As you're surrounded by thick vegetation, it's sometimes hard to see the animals on this fascinating walk in the woods with a difference. The gorillas are the main attraction, but if the stars of the show prove shy, you can also spot

hippos, birds, and even some mole-rats.

5 Festival of The Lion King

One of Orlando's best shows, this spectacle won't fail to throw you into the spirit of things. The production features singers, dancers, and *The Lion King*'s popular score to emphasize nature's diversity.

6 DINOSAUR

Expect to be shaken up on this ride, which takes you back 65 million years. Convincing anima-tronic dinosaurs lurk in the darkness. You need to be 40 inches (102 cm).

7 It's Tough to Be a Bug!®

Located inside the Tree of Life's 50-ft (15-m) base, this 3D, effect-filled show offers a view

of the world from an insect's perspective.

8 The Boneyard®

Possibly the best playground in any of the parks, this dinosaur dig site is perfect for kids.

9 Finding Nemo: The Big Blue... and Beyond!

The Theater in the Wild® is transformed into an enchanted undersea world for this original 30-minute stage show, which merges puppetry with live performances.

10 Kali River Rapids®

The park's conservation message is evident on this raft ride, which passes from a lush landscape to one in the process of being scorched for logging.

> **PARK GUIDE**
> Maps are available at the park entrance. The exciting after-dark experiences include the Tree of Life Awakenings, and Disney Kite Tails, plus character cavalcades that spontaneously pop up and float down Discovery River. Pandora – The World of Avatar also brings the movie's spectac-ular bioluminescent landscapes to life at night.

Exploring Pandora – The World of Avatar

UNIVERSAL STUDIOS FLORIDA™

📍 T1 📍 1000 Universal Studios Plaza 🕐 9am–7pm daily, with extended seasonal hours 🌐 universalorlando.com ↗

Elaborately designed streetscapes and innovative special effects bring the silver screen to life in this movie and TV studio theme park. Immerse yourself in your favorite movies and shows as you ride with the Simpsons, save the world with the Transformers, or party with the Minions.

Race Through New York Starring Jimmy Fallon

1 Race Through New York Starring Jimmy Fallon

A 3D motion simulator has guests join chat show host Jimmy Fallon as he races along various New York landmarks.

2 Hollywood Rip Ride Rockit®

Choose your own soundtrack on this 65-mph (105-km/h) coaster, which towers 17 stories above Universal, spills into CityWalk™, and has a record-breaking loop.

3 Fast & Furious: Supercharged™

Feel your heart pound as you ride these full-throttle, high-octane vehicles alongside Dom, Letty, Hobbs, and the rest of the *Fast & Furious* crew.

4 Despicable Me Minion Mayhem

Explore the lair and secret lab of super-villain Gru in this interactive 3D digital adventure. Riders are transformed into Minions and taken to a Minion dance party.

5 E.T. Adventure®

Everyone's favorite alien takes guests on a bike ride to save his planet. Pedal through strange landscapes to meet Tickli Moot Moot and other characters created by Steven Spielberg especially for this ride.

6 Revenge of the Mummy®

This thrilling high-speed coaster propels riders backward and forward through ancient Egyptian tombs to face their deepest fears, heightened by darkness, as Imhotep unleashes his wrath.

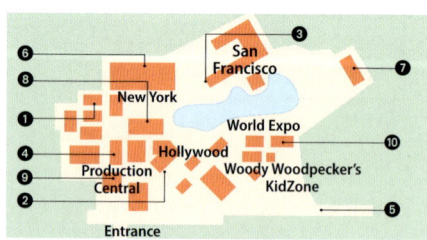

Universal Studios Florida™ Site Plan

Battling villains in Illumination's Villain-Con Minion Blast

TOP TIP

Buy the Universal Express™ Pass in order to reduce wait times.

7 MEN IN BLACK™ Alien Attack™

You and your "alienator" must keep the intergalactic bad guys from taking over the world as you spin through the streets, looking to shoot monstrous bugs.

8 Transformers: The Ride-3D

This action-packed ride, based on the popular movies, includes 60-ft- (18-m-) tall 3D robots.

9 Illumination's Villain-Con Minion Blast

Guests use lasers to blast their way along a slowly moving walkway, avoiding the Vicious 6 and hitting targets to attain supervillain stardom.

10 The Simpsons Ride™

Swoop, soar, and smash your way through Krustyland on an exciting motion simulator ride with Bart and the rest of this well-loved U.S. cartoon family.

PARK GUIDE
It takes about 20 minutes to get from the parking lot to the attractions. If you're staying at a Universal hotel, use the early admission perk; otherwise, try to arrive early and hit the major rides first. The on-site hotels also offer guests complimentary transportation to the parks.

Characters at The Simpsons Ride™

Kids' Attractions

1. Kang and Kodos Twirl 'n' Hurl
This kid-friendly Simpsons-inspired ride defies its name to take riders gently up and down while spinning round. Think Dumbo the Flying Elephant at the Magic Kingdom® *(p22)*, but with an edgy twist.

2. Trolls Trollercoaster
Opened in 2024, this family coaster passes your favorite Trolls characters along the track and is suitable for younger children.

3. Animal Actors on Location
A creative animal show featuring wild, wacky, and occasionally weird live and video animal action. Expect plenty of audience participation.

4. Po Live
This state-of-the-art, interactive digital exhibit was launched in 2024 as part of Po's Kung Fu Training Camp in DreamWorks Land.

5. ¡Vamos! – Báilalo!
A high-energy, interactive show staged between Louie's Italian Restaurant and Starbucks, showcasing Latin American music and dance moves.

6. The Blues Brothers®
Fans of the movie, starring John Belushi and Dan Ackroyd, will enjoy this foot-stomping 20-minute revue.

Live-action Bourne Stuntacular show

7. The Bourne Stuntacular
Follow Jason Bourne through the dangerous world of spies, espionage, and government secrets in this action-packed stunt show, which combines stagecraft and film.

8. Universal's Superstar Parade™
Themed floats, street performers, and larger-than-life characters – including Spongebob Squarepants, Dora and Diego, Gru, Agnes, Edith, Margo, and the Minions – get the party started through the streets of Universal Studios Florida™.

9. Drive In and Dance
This 1950s-themed dance show takes place in the plaza space in front of Mel's Drive-In. It's perfect for all ages.

10. Universal Orlando's Horror Makeup Show™
A hilarious and educational look at special effects makeup used in the movies. Universal unveils the industry secrets with movie clips, props, and demonstrations.

The Blues Brothers® show at Universal Studios Florida™

BEHIND THE SCENES

TOP 10
MOVIES MADE
AT UNIVERSAL
STUDIOS FLORIDA™

1. Psycho IV *(1990)*
2. The Waterboy *(1998)*
3. Hoover *(1998)*
4. House on Haunted Hill *(1999)*
5. Beethoven's Big Break *(2008)*
6. Ace Ventura Jr *(2009)*
7. The Final Destination *(2009)*
8. The Renee Project *(2011)*
9. Tooth Fairy 2 *(2011)*
10. Sharknado 3 *(2015)*

Kung Fu Panda: The Emperor's Quest at DreamWorks Theatre

Universal Studios Florida™ is more than just a tourist attraction. Since opening in 1990, it has also been the production site for thousands of television shows, commercials, music videos, and movies. While TV and movie production has been scaled back in favor of theme park rides and live entertainment (such as Hard Rock Live at Universal CityWalk™), there are still six sound stages, two event stages, broadcast studios, casting and makeup services, post-production editing facilities, and various back-lot film sets, including re-creations of New York City streets, Hollywood Boulevard, and many others. Though these areas are not normally open to the public, if park guests want to be part of some camera action, they can join the studio audience when TV shows shoot episodes at Universal. Tickets for these productions are typically distributed free of charge on the day of taping at the Studio Audience Center, located near Guest Services. Note that tickets are issued on a first-come, first-served basis. Visitors can check in advance with Guest Services to find out if special-event TV shows will be taped during their visit.

UNIVERSAL'S ISLANDS OF ADVENTURE™

T1 · **Hollywood Way** · **9am–6pm, with extended seasonal hours**
w universalorlando.com

Orlando didn't have a lot to offer adrenaline junkies until Universal unveiled its second Central Florida park in 1999. Universal's Islands of Adventure™ brought immersive settings filled with thrilling attractions, including terrifying roller coasters and heart-stopping water rides.

1 Dudley Do-Right's Ripsaw Falls®

Expect to get wet on this thrilling flume ride. Dudley's adventure peaks with a 75-ft (23-m) drop at speeds reaching 50 mph (80 km/h) – you'll then plummet some 15 ft (4.5 m) below the water's surface (albeit safely behind glass) before the ride's end.

2 Pteranodon Flyers®

Eye-catching metal gondolas swing from side to side on this prehistoric bird's-eye tour around the Jurassic Park zone.

3 The Amazing Adventures of Spider-Man®

Put on 3D glasses and battle the villains while fireballs and other high-definition objects fly at you in this 3D motion simulator. The experience is truly amazing.

> **EAT**
> Meet and dine with your favorite super-heroes, including Captain America and Spider-Man, at the Marvel Character Diner. Book ahead.

Universal's Islands of Adventure™ Site Plan

4 Popeye & Bluto's Bilge-Rat Barges

Another less intense water ride, this time aboard a 12-person raft going through white-water rapids. Watch out for the water cannons that fire at the rafts.

5 Poseidon's Fury®

The line for this ride takes you through eerie ruins, setting the scene for the special effects show. A thrilling 42-ft (13-m) vortex of water forms a projection screen

Meeting Spider-Man at the theme park

Spectacular Skull Island: Reign of Kong ride

for the epic battle between titans Poseidon and Lord Darkenon.

6 Jurassic Park River Adventure®

This ride starts slow, but picks up speed as raptors get loose. Take the 85-ft- (26-m-) flume-style plunge to escape.

7 The Cat in the Hat™

Pace yourself as your couch spins and turns through 18 Seussian scenes. The Cat, Thing One, and Thing Two join you on the ride.

8 Incredible Hulk Coaster®

One of the biggest thrills in the park. Blast out of the darkness at up to 67 mph (108 km/h), go weightless, and endure inversions and drops.

Up close with the Jurassic World raptors, VelociCoaster

9 Skull Island: Reign of Kong

Vehicles take you deep into the ruins of Skull Island for an intense encounter with fierce beasts, prehistoric predators, gigantic bugs, and Kong himself.

10 VelociCoaster

Twist, turn, and speed through jungle terrain to escape pre-historic velociraptors on this Jurassic World themed ride.

PARK GUIDE
It can take 20 minutes to get to the park from the parking lot. Arrive early; any-one staying at a Universal resort can enter before other visitors. Guests at the Royal Pacific, Hard Rock, and Loews Portofino Bay Hotel also get free Universal Express Access (otherwise from $39.99).

Enjoying the Flight of the Hippogriff™ roller coaster

Gentler Attractions

1. Flight of the Hippogriff™
This family-friendly roller coaster dives into the Forbidden Forest, and then weaves its way past the pumpkin patch and Hagrid's hut.

2. Jurassic Park® Discovery Center
See through a dinosaur's eyes, match your DNA to theirs, and watch an animatronic velociraptor "hatch" in the laboratory. There are several interactive stations, where kids can brush up on their dinosaur knowledge.

3. Caro-Seuss-el™
Dr. Seuss's cowfish, elephant birds, and mulligatawnies replace traditional horses at this unique merry-go-round.

4. If I Ran the Zoo™
The 19 interactive stations in this Seussian playground include flying water snakes, caves, and water cannons, as well as a place to tickle the toes of a Seussian critter.

5. One Fish, Two Fish, Red Fish, Blue Fish™
Fly your fish up, down, and all around on an aerial carousel ride just 15 ft (4 m) off the ground. Get sprayed with water if you don't follow the song.

6. High in the Sky Seuss Trolley Train Ride!™
Follow the story of the Sneetches™ on this gentle ride above the attractions of Seuss Landing.

7. Camp Jurassic™
Explore this playground full of intriguing places, including dark caves where "spitters" (small dinosaurs) lurk.

8. Me Ship, The Olive®
The play area here is full of interactive fun, while Cargo Crane offers an alternative hands-on experience: a chance to fire water cannons at riders on Popeye & Bluto's Bilge-Rat Barges *(p38)*.

9. The Mystic Fountain
Make a wish at this fountain in Sinbad's Village. It's surprisingly playful, asking questions of and teasing guests.

10. Storm Force Accelatron®
Spin your vehicle fast enough with X-Men superhero Storm to create enough electrical energy to send the villainous Magneto to the great beyond.

"STATE-OF-THE-FUTURE" RIDES

Guests at Universal's Islands of Adventure™ get a first-hand demonstration of some of the most technologically advanced attractions ever created. The Amazing Adventures of Spider-Man® *(p38)* took five years and more than $100 million to develop. New digital film technologies had to be invented for the floor-to-ceiling 3D images projected to a moving audience. The motion simulator, wind cannons, and pyrotechnics are all synchronized by a vast computer network. For the immersive experience of Reign of Kong *(p39)*, screens create a seamless tunnel of realistic 3D imagery across the high-tech vehicles, which together with next-generation technology puts riders right in the middle of the action. Unique to the Incredible Hulk Coaster® *(p39)* is a thrust system that catapults the sleek cars out of a specially designed tunnel rather than the usual long, slow haul to the top of an incline. Even so, some low-tech touches can't be avoided: just below is a huge net to catch the belongings that fall from screaming riders.

Riders hanging on as the Incredible Hulk Coaster® increasingly gathers speed

7

THE WIZARDING WORLD OF HARRY POTTER™

📍 T1 🏠 Hogsmeade™: Universal's Islands of Adventure™; Diagon Alley™: Universal Studios Florida™ 🕐 9am–6pm daily, with extended seasonal hours 🌐 universalorlando.com ↗

Walk around Diagon Alley™, travel into Gringotts™ bank, choose a wand at Ollivanders™: it's all possible at The Wizarding World of Harry Potter™. Spread across two parks – Universal's Islands of Adventure™ and Universal Studios Florida™ – and connected by the Hogwarts™ Express, this fun-filled world is a must-visit for fans.

1 Harry Potter and the Escape from Gringotts™

Even the line for this thrill ride through the underground vaults of Gringotts™ bank raises a smile – you enter through a grand lobby of diligently working goblins. The ride itself combines coaster and simulator as you evade the bank's security, not to mention Bellatrix and Voldemort. Note that this is the only ride in Diagon Alley™.

2 Flight of the Hippogriff™

This family-friendly coaster (*p40*) introduces you to the Hippogriff and takes you on a training flight around the pumpkin patch and Hagrid's Hut.

3 Spell Casting – Interactive Wand Experiences

There are interactive wands on sale at Ollivanders™, which produce various effects when swished or flicked at locations marked on the included map.

Diagon Alley™ Site Plan

TOP TIP

The Universal Express™ Pass offers access to all rides and attractions here.

The colorful streets of Diagon Alley™

Knockturn Alley for darker objects at Borgin and Burkes™ *(p113)*.

5 Harry Potter and the Forbidden Journey™

The line takes you on a tour through Hogwarts, before you soar over the grounds in this simulator ride. Riders get tossed around, and come face to face with Dementors.

6 The Knight Bus™

Parked just outside Diagon Alley™ is the triple-decker Knight Bus™, where you can chat with the conductor.

7 Hogwarts™ Express

Guests with multi-park passes can travel between parks aboard this steam train, with regular departures from both King's Cross and Hogsmeade™ stations. Once the doors close on your compartment, you'll

DRINK
Sample some frothy, creamy, and tasty butterbeer (served cold, warm, or frozen) at the Three Broomstichs, the Leaky Cauldron, or a quich-stop cart.

4 Shopping in Diagon Alley™

Pick up Quidditch equipment, robes, chocolate frogs, even extendable ears from the shops here, including Weasleys' Wizard Wheezes™. Turn into

Hogsmeade™ Site Plan

whiz through the scenic English countryside; Ron, Hermione, and Harry are on board, too.

8 The Nighttime Lights at Hogwarts™ Castle

On select nights, Hogsmeade™ village comes to life with special effects, music, and lights in a celebration of the four houses of Hogwarts. At nightfall, watch the spirit of each house wrap itself around the castle.

9 Street Performances

Watch live singers and puppet shows based on *The Tales of Beedle the Bard*. Hogsmeade™ showcases the Frog Choir, while Durmstrang and Beauxbatons students perform in the Triwizard Spirit Rally at Hogwarts.

10 Ollivanders™

At this interactive experience, the wand chooses the wizard. Both Ollivanders™ wand shops are spectacular, but Diagon Alley's is bigger, and has shorter lines.

The Weasleys' Wizard Wheezes™ store

8

LEGOLAND®

B2 · 1000 Universal Studios Plaza · 9am–7pm, with extended seasonal hours · universalorlando.com ·

This kid-friendly theme park opened in 2011, to the delight of children and big kids alike. Like its counterparts around the world, it features larger-than-life LEGO® creations (along with thousands of smaller models), and more than 50 LEGO® – and DUPLO® – based rides, shows, and attractions. Kids can fly, drive, build, and climb their way through miniature cities, medieval kingdoms, and Egyptian ruins.

1 DUPLO® Valley
Little children can board the DUPLO® Train to explore the countryside, look for missing farm animals on the DUPLO® Tractor ride, cool off in the DUPLO® Splash and Play area, or climb around the DUPLO® Farm play area.

2 The Great LEGO® Race
In this race set in a virtual world, compete against a number of LEGO® minifigures while riding a roller coaster. Experience the action from every direction – up, down, forward, and backward.

3 The Dragon
Ride high above the park's version of a medieval village in a

Enjoying the play area at DUPLO® Valley

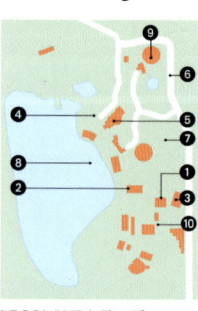

LEGOLAND® Site Plan

**Main entrance
to LEGOLAND®**

🛍 **SHOP**
There are
plenty of shops
around the park for
those looking to buy
more LEGO. For the
ultimate shopping
experience, head
to The Big Shop.

dragon-themed coaster,
twisting and turning both
indoors and out, along a
track that winds its way
through the enchanted
LEGOLAND® Castle.

4 Botanical Gardens

First planted in 1936,
these gardens were
preserved as part
LEGOLAND®. See an
array of plants, including
a huge banyan tree.

5 Imagination Zone

Filled with activities that
encourage creativity, this
zone allows kids to design
their own cutting-edge
robots, play the latest
LEGO® video games, or
build creations with real
or virtual LEGO® blocks.

6 Flying School

With their feet
dangling freely, riders
will seemingly fly
through the air (or at
least along the track)
on this suspended roller
coaster ride. The Flying
School opens later

**Plummeting down a slide,
LEGOLAND® Water Park**

than the park in the
morning on select dates
throughout the year.

7 Coastersaurus

Ride this old-
fashioned wooden roller
coaster, in the Land of
Adventure, as it zooms
through a prehistoric
forest with slow curves
and dips. Life-sized
LEGO® creatures peep
out from the foliage.

8 Pirate's Cove Live Water Ski Show

This 20-minute live-
action show entertains
the crowds with water-
skiers, jet-skiers, boats,
and pyrotechnic special
effects, as guards seek
to protect the ship
Brickbeard's Bounty
from marauding pirates.

9 LEGOLAND® Water Park

Located next to the
theme park (and ticketed
separately), LEGOLAND®
Water Park offers plenty
of attractions for cooling
off on a hot day, including
a wave pool, lazy river,
and numerous splash and
play areas.

10 LEGO® Movies in 4D

A variety of 4D produc-
tions, including a NEXO
Knights movie and The
LEGO® Movie, are shown
in a 700-seat theater.
Kids will love the multi-
sensory movies.

🛈 **PARK GUIDE**
On entering
the park, pick up
a map and one
of the handy show
guides available
at Guest Services.
Check show times,
character meet-and-
greets, and operating
hours of the rides to
ensure you can fit
everything into your
time at the park.

Larger-than-Life LEGO® Creations

The LEGO® Ferrari Build and Race area of the park

1. Ferrari 296 GTS

Unveiled in 2024, this life-sized luxury car is made almost entirely of LEGO® (it has real tires). Visitors can jump in the driver's seat to get a picture.

2. U.S. Capitol Building

One of the standout creations in Miniland U.S.A., LEGO®'s version of the U.S. Capitol Building is also one of the most popular. It features a towering dome and an intricately columned facade; those with eagle eyes will also spot the moving marching band figures at the front of the building.

3. Empire State Building

Even though most of Miniland U.S.A. is built to a 1:20 scale, the skyscrapers are something to behold. The most iconic one is New York's famous Empire State Building, which measures 20 ft (7 m) tall, making it one of the tallest models in the park.

4. Kennedy Space Center Visitor Complex

Can't make it to the real Kennedy Space Center Visitor Complex *(p52)*? See the mini model in LEGOLAND® instead. This vast construction features a Space Shuttle ready for launch, plus an impressive re-creation of the Space Garden and Vehicle Assembly Building.

5. Daytona International Speedway

This incredible sporting arena took almost 300,000 bricks and a team of a dozen Master Model Builders working for 2,100 hours to re-create. It's an atmospheric model, featuring the sounds of roaring engines and cheering crowds.

6. Pirate Shores

A tropical lagoon complete with magnificent tall ships is one of the few scenes in the park not based on real life. It's easy to imagine plenty of swashbuckling fun on the high seas.

7. Hollywood Bowl

California landmarks are well represented in Miniland U.S.A. Visitors can get up close to the Golden Gate Bridge and the Griffith Observatory, but the Hollywood Bowl takes the cake with its model orchestra entertaining a captivated LEGO® crowd.

8. The Vegas Strip

Real-life Las Vegas specializes in replica landmarks (the Nevada city hosts a model Eiffel Tower and Venetian canals), and LEGO®'s version is no different. Marvel at the Luxor Pyramid, the Stratosphere Tower and the Strip's most iconic buildings.

9. Florida

Even if you're just visiting Orlando, it's easy to see the rest of the Sunshine State here (or at least some of its more famous spots). Gaze at the grand mansions of the Panhandle or take a look at Mallory Square in Key West.

10. Ford F-150 Lightning

This hulking truck arrived in LEGOLAND® in 2022 with a full-size truck bed, and working headlights and taillights. It's on permanent display outside the LEGOLAND® Driving School.

**Ole Kirk Christiansen,
founder of the
LEGO® company.**

THE HISTORY OF LEGO®

Founded by Danish carpenter Ole Kirk Christiansen in the 1930s, LEGO® was named after the Danish phrase "leg godt," meaning "play well." The company's toys were initially made of wood but with the invention of plastic moulding in the 1940s, production soon switched to plastic. In 1949, the first building bricks were sold and in 1958 the LEGO® brick as we know it today was patented. Sales continued to soar throughout the 1960s and '70s, with the brand quickly becoming a global phenomenon. During this time, technical and specialist models such as pirates and space-themed kits became available, taking the LEGO® experience to the next level. With such success, it was time to expand beyond mini-models: the first LEGO® park opened in Billund, Denmark in 1968, with the second following in Windsor, UK, in 1996. LEGOLAND® reached the states at the turn of the century, touching down in Carlsbad, California, in 1999. The Orlando outpost opened its gates in 2011 and has been drawing fans of the brand ever since.

LEGO® MOVIE WORLD™ at Orlando's LEGOLAND®

9

MERRITT ISLAND

X5 | East of Titusville on SR 402 | Apr–Oct: 9am–4pm Mon–Sat; Nov–Mar: 9am–4pm daily | Federal hols | fws.gov/refuge/merritt_island

Merritt Island National Wildlife Refuge at the Kennedy Space Center Visitor Complex has become the second-largest reserve in Florida. Founded in 1963 to serve as a buffer zone for NASA, its 219 sq miles (567 sq km) now provide an important habitat for endangered species and a vital stopover along the migration path of hundreds of birds. The manatees are the refuge's most popular attraction.

1 Boating
Boating or canoeing is the best way to get close to the wildlife. In season, the waterways are filled with wading birds at migratory pit stops and manatees in the depths.

2 Fishing
With both Florida State and Refuge fishing permits, you can cast your line on the Indian River, Banana River, and Mosquito Lagoon. Red drum, spotted sea trout, and snook are the most common catches.

3 Visitor Center
In addition to a 20-minute video, the center has exhibits and displays providing a good introduction to the island. The ponds behind the center are favorite spots for alligators.

TOP TIP

Alligators move quickly on land – exercise caution when viewing them.

4 Black Point Wildlife Drive
The best places to spot wildlife here are linked by road. Follow the 7-mile (11-km), one-way loop to see waterfowl, wading birds, and raptors.

5 Manatee Observation Deck
Most common in spring and fall, manatees frequent the refuge year-round. See them up close in Banana River or from the viewing platform at Haulover Canal.

Clockwise from top
**Observatory at
Merritt Island
National Wildlife
Refuge; strolling on
a boardwalk trail in
the refuge; the
park's visitor center**

6 Bird Tours
The reserve organizes excellent bird-watching tours for beginners, where park volunteers will help you identify many of the different species in the refuge.

7 Pine Island Conservation Area
The marshland preserve has hiking trails that lead through pine flatwoods, mangrove forests, and along the salt marsh habitats. There are kayaking and canoeing opportunities, as well as dedicated cycling trails.

8 Hiking
There are seven hiking trails on offer. Most are quite wet, but none are too strenuous. They range from a quarter of a mile (0.4 km) to 5 miles (8 km).

9 Beaches
Visitors to the refuge spend more time on land than in water, but Playalinda Beach provides access, parking, and other facilities for swimmers. Beware of alligators on the road to the beach.

10 Migrations
All year round, the refuge plays host to migrating animals. The birds return in May, and in June and July turtles lay eggs on the beaches. Waterfowl abound on rivers in September.

Relaxing on a white-sand beach at Merritt Island

Flock of white ibis on Merritt Island

KENNEDY SPACE CENTER VISITOR COMPLEX

X5 Rte 405, Titusville 9am–5pm daily kennedyspacecenter.com

Still the site of spacecraft launches, the Kennedy Space Center Visitor Complex is one of Florida's most popular tourist destinations. Its host of exhibits, live rocket launches, and encounters with astronauts gives everyone a chance to experience their own space adventure and provides a lovely alternative to a day at a theme park.

1 Apollo/Saturn V Center

Visitors can relive the historic launch of Apollo 8 in the Firing Room Theater, and walk underneath one of only three Saturn V (p54) rockets left in existence.

2 Gateway: The Deep Space Launch Complex

See innovative space technologies and the future of space exploration before entering this spaceport ride.

Saturn V rocket, the Apollo/Saturn V Center

TOP TIP

Rochet launch tickets must be bought in advance (877 313 2610).

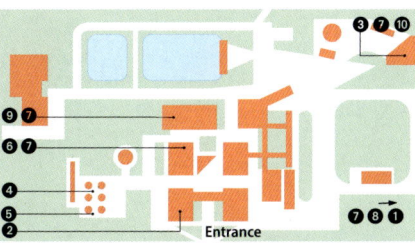

Kennedy Space Center Visitor Complex Site Plan

The Kennedy Space
Center Visitor Complex

EAT
Grab a tasty
hot dog and sit next
to a piece of rock
from the moon at
the Moon Rock Café.

3 Shuttle Launch Experience

This exciting simulation ride allows all visitors to the center to experience the unique sights, sounds, and sensations of a space shuttle launch.

4 Rocket Garden

Unlike any other garden you have seen, this area has eight real spacecraft, including a Mercury Atlas. Red, white, and blue lighting adds drama to these rockets.

5 Heroes & Legends

Experience the dawn of the Space Age and meet the heroes in the U.S. Astronaut Hall of Fame. Visitors can journey through space and time in a 4D theater, and get a close-up view of the Gemini 9 capsule.

6 Journey to Mars

This attraction combines a live presentation with multimedia exhibits and simulators – a reminder that the future of space exploration relies on humanity's drive and innovation.

7 Cosmic Quest

Purchase a one-day badge and it's game on. This live action gaming attraction allows players to experience four different immersive astronaut adventures alongside Robonaut, a remarkably dexterous humanoid robot.

8 KSC Explore Tours

Visitors are treated to an insider's view of the center. Drive by launch pads and disembark for photos at the picturesque NASA Causeway and Vehicle Assembly Building.

9 IMAX – Science on a Sphere

The center's twin, back-to-back, 5.5-story theaters show two movies: *Journey to Space*, which explores NASA's plans for deep space exploration, and *A Beautiful Planet*, showing stunning images of the Earth's surface.

10 Space Shuttle Atlantis

Admire a close-up view of the Atlantis displayed here in mid-flight glory. There are more than 60 interactive exhibits.

CENTER GUIDE
About a 55-minute drive from Orlando, the Kennedy Space Center Visitor Complex is located within the Merritt Island National Wildlife Refuge (*p48*). Admission includes a bus tour with a view of a launch pad and the Apollo 8 launch site, ending at the Apollo/Saturn V Center. Board the bus tour inside the complex, through the information center.

Rockets: Past, Present, and Future

The Saturn 1B on display in the Rocket Garden

1. Jupiter C
This early variation of the Mercury Redstone rocket was developed by a team headed by the German scientist Wernher von Braun. The Jupiter C carried the U.S.'s first satellite, Explorer I, which launched on January 31, 1958.

2. X-15
The X-15 rocket plane flew 199 missions from 1959 to 1968, carrying a who's who of astronauts, including moon-walker Neil Armstrong. It reached altitudes of 354,200 ft (107,960 m) and speeds of 4,520 mph (7,274 km/h).

3. Mercury Redstone
This rocket carried the first American into space. Alan B. Shepard Jr.'s 15-minute, 22-second ride aboard the Freedom 7 capsule in 1961 was one of six flights in the Mercury program.

4. Mercury Atlas
When the six-flight Mercury program graduated from sub-orbital to orbital flights, the Atlas replaced the Mercury Redstone. It was this rocket that took John H. Glenn Jr., Scott Carpenter, Wally Schirra, and Gordon Cooper into space in 1962 and 1963.

5. Titan II
When a larger capsule was needed for two-person crews, this rocket earned its place in NASA history. It was used for a total of 10 crewed flights (Gemini Titan expeditions) in 1965 and 1966.

6. Saturn 1B
The Saturn 1B launched Apollo lunar spacecraft into Earth's orbit in the mid-1960s, in training for crewed flights to the moon. Later, it launched three missions to get a crew at the Skylab space station (1973), as well as the American crew for the Apollo/Soyuz Test Project (1975).

7. Saturn V
At 363 ft (110 m), this was the largest launch vehicle ever produced. The highlight of its career was Apollo 11, the three-astronaut mission that famously landed Buzz Aldrin and Neil Armstrong on the moon on July 20, 1969.

8. Titan Centaur
The Titan Centaur rocket launched Voyager I and II in 1977, on a historic mission to explore Jupiter, Saturn, Uranus, and – 12 years after its launch – Neptune.

9. Pegasus
Today's version of this winged wonder is capable of flying small communications satellites into a low Earth orbit from the bellies of mother ships, such as the L-1011.

10. Falcon 9
Designed and manufactured by SpaceX, Falcon 9 is the world's first orbital class reusable rocket. The two-stage rocket was created to safely transport both people and payloads.

TOP 10
U.S. CREWED SPACE
PROGRAM EVENTS

1. May 5, 1961: Alan B. Shepard Jr. becomes the first American in space.

2. Feb 20, 1962: John H. Glenn Jr. becomes the first American to orbit the Earth.

3. Jun 3, 1965: Edward H. White Jr. becomes the first American to walk in space.

4. Jul 20, 1969: Neil Armstrong becomes the first person to walk on the moon.

5. Apr 11–13, 1970: An explosion nearly causes disaster for Apollo 13.

6. Apr 12, 1981: The first shuttle is launched.

7. Jan 28, 1986: Seven die in the Challenger space shuttle explosion.

8. May 27–Jun 6, 1999: The space shuttle docks for the first time at the International Space Station.

9. Jul 21, 2011: The groundbreaking shuttle program ends with the landing of Endeavour at Kennedy Space Center.

10. April 23, 2021: The Falcon 9 blasts into space with four crew members, the first crewed rocket from the U.S. since the shuttle program ended.

THE SPACE SHUTTLE

The space shuttles were the first fully reusable spacecraft and the best recognized of NASA's vehicles. Five of them ventured into space: Columbia, Challenger, Discovery, Atlantis, and Endeavour. Once in orbit, the shuttles were capable of cruising at 17,500 mph (28,163 km/h), and their cargo bays could hold a fully loaded tour bus, yet the engineless orbiters could glide to a runway more gracefully than a pelican landing on water. Two of the spacecraft – the Challenger in 1986 and Columbia in 2003 – broke down, leading to the deaths of all the crew members on board. Despite these massive tragedies, the shuttles were a remarkable success. They were pivotal in building the International Space Station and extending the life of the Hubble Space Telescope, and their crews carried out valuable cutting-edge research while in orbit.

Taking a photo in front of the NASA globe with a space shuttle rising behind

TOP 10 OF EVERYTHING

Museums	58
Cultural Venues	60
Thrill Rides	62
Smaller Attractions	64
Parks and Preserves	66
Places to Cool Off	70
Spas	72
Sports and Outdoor Activities	74
Golf Courses	76
Off the Beaten Path	78
Live Music Venues	80
Favorite LGBTQ+ Spots	82
Dining Experiences	84
Places to Shop	86
Orlando for Free	88
Festivals and Events	90
Day Trips South and West	92
Day Trips North and East	94

Riding a roller coaster in Busch Gardens®

MUSEUMS

1 Orlando Museum of Art
The Orlando Museum of Art (OMA) is one of the Southeast's top arts museums *(p123)*. The permanent collection here is dominated by pre-Columbian art and American artists. These are supplemented by touring exhibitions from major metropolitan museums, and numerous smaller shows of regional or local significance.

2 Orlando Science Center
A huge, attention-grabbing, exploratorium-style museum *(p123)*, the Orlando Science Center has hundreds of interactive, child-friendly exhibits designed to introduce kids to the wonders of science. Its ten themed zones deal with subjects ranging from mechanics to math, health and fitness to lasers. Don't miss the CineDome, which accommodates a planetarium and the world's largest Iwerks® theater.

3 Mennello Museum of American Art
This lakeside museum *(p124)* houses an unusual collection of paintings by obscure curio shop owner and Floridian folk artist Earl Cunningham (1893–1977). In addition to his own work, there are traveling exhibitions that feature the works of other "outsider" artists.

4 Orange County Regional History Center
Housed in a 1927 courthouse, this museum *(p125)* crams 12,000 years of Central Florida's past into three floors. Exhibits include local photographs and memorabilia as well as a re-created Victorian parlor, a 1926 fire station, and fascinating temporary shows that cover themes such as pirates and space travel.

5 Rollins Museum of Art
Located on the campus of Rollins College, this small, stylish

Interactive exhibit at Orlando Science Center

Nick Cave's *Soundsuit*, Orlando Museum of Art

museum *(p131)* is one of Florida's oldest art collections. It showcases European and American paintings, sculpture, and decorative arts from the Renaissance and Baroque periods to the 20th century. Highlights include *Madonna and Child Enthroned* (c.1480) by Cosimo Rosselli, and *Reclining Figure* (1982) by Henry Moore.

6 Holocaust Memorial Resource & Education Center

🔲 J3 🏠 851 N. Maitland Ave ⏰ 9am–4pm Mon–Thu, 9am–1pm Fri, 1–4pm Sun 🌐 holocaustedu.org

Founded in 1980 by Holocaust survivors and witnesses, the memorial aims to generate compassion and generosity in future generations. The museum conducts lectures, hosts a film series, and has a permanent exhibition of remembrances.

7 Charles Hosmer Morse Museum of American Art

This museum *(p131)* displays the world's most comprehensive collection of work by American artist Louis Comfort Tiffany, best known for his Art Nouveau stained glass. Highlights include a chapel made for the 1893 World's Columbian Exposition and a re-creation of Tiffany's legendary New York home.

Loving Cup, Charles Hosmer Morse Museum of American Art

8 Albin Polasek Museum and Sculpture Gardens

Czech-American sculptor Polasek (1879–1965) was famed for creating landmark public monuments across Chicago. These gardens are filled with his work, as are the four galleries at this self-designed house and studio *(p131)*.

9 The Grand Bohemian Gallery

🔲 P3 🏠 325 S. Orange Ave ⏰ Hours vary, check website 🌐 grand bohemiangallery.com

The Grand Bohemian Hotel displays over 150 works by local, regional, and internationally acclaimed artists. Pieces include jewelry, glassware, and paintings.

10 Art & History Museums of Maitland

🔲 J4 🏠 221 & 231 W. Packwood Ave ⏰ 11am–4pm Thu–Sun 🌐 artand history.org

Artifacts, textiles, and photos from Maitland's pioneer days are the focus here. The Maitland Art Center is one of the few remainders of Mayan Revival Architecture, while the Telephone Museum has a selection of vintage phones and memorabilia.

CULTURAL VENUES

Seating at the arthouse cinema Enzian

1 Osceola Arts

Kissimmee's home of high culture offers a theater, art gallery, and a variety of special events. Osceola Arts (p120) has an engagingly diverse schedule, eagerly offering a little bit of everything, from Broadway to barbershop, and storytelling to sculptures.

2 The Orlando Family Stage

📍 M3 🏠 1001 E. Princeton St
🌐 orlandofamilystage.com 🔗

Founded as the Orlando Little Theatre in 1926, this wonderful venue has evolved into Orlando's only full-time professional theater for young audiences. Broadway performances are offered throughout the year, with past productions including *Junie B. Jones*, Disney's *Little Mermaid*, and *Mary Poppins*.

3 Bob Carr Theatre

📍 P2 🏠 401 W. Livingston St
🌐 bobcarrperformingartscenter. net 🔗

Open since the 1920s, this theater is home to both the Orlando Philharmonic Orchestra and the Florida Symphony Youth Orchestra. With a capacity of 2,500, it's a favorite among classical music fans.

4 Orlando Philharmonic

📍 N4 🏠 425 N. Bumby Ave
🌐 orlandophil.org 🔗

Orlando's resident orchestra has more than 80 conservatory-trained musicians. Venues vary, but include the Phil's home at The Plaza Live, the Bob Carr Theatre, and the Dr. Phillips Center for the Performing Arts. It puts on a variety of concert series, from pop to classical and opera.

5 SAK Comedy Lab

📍 P3 🏠 29 S. Orange Ave
🌐 sakcomedylab.com 🔗

A Downtown favorite, SAK is Orlando's home of improvisation comedy. Shows are always funny and inventive, and there are two per night. The 8pm shows are usually family-friendly, while the later ones get a bit edgier, although obscene material is strictly avoided. Of particular interest are the series shows, such as *Foolish Hearts*, an ongoing, improvised soap opera.

6 Enzian Theater

Central Florida's only full-time arthouse cinema, Enzian (p132) is a

Adventures of Pericles **performance at Orlando Shakes**

unique venue – its single-screen, 250-seat house is arranged like a dinner theater, with waitstaff serving food and drinks (including beer and wine). It screens foreign and American indie classics, and hosts regular special-interest festivals, like the Florida Film Festival *(p90)*.

7 Orlando International Fringe Festival

Held at the Lowndes Shakespeare Center, the Orlando Rep, and other nearby sites, the 14-day Orlando Fringe *(p90)* follows in the footsteps of the granddaddy of fringe: the Edinburgh Fringe in Scotland. It presents uncensored, unjuried music, dance, and other performances, and 100 percent of box office sales go to the artists.

8 Orlando Ballet
M3 **415 E. Princeton St**
orlandoballet.org

This is the only fully residential ballet company in Central Florida. It presents four major productions annually, including a version of *The Nutcracker* as well as special performances throughout the year. Smaller shows are held on community stages, with productions at the Dr. Phillips Center for the Performing Arts.

9 Orlando Shakes
M3 **812 E. Rollins St**
orlandoshakes.org

This nationally recognized theater company performs modern classics and Broadway hits, as well as lots of the Bard's works. Its productions can be seen in an eight-month-long season at its theater at Loch Haven Park.

10 Dr. Phillips Center for the Performing Arts
P3 **445 S. Magnolia Ave**
drphillipscenter.org

This high-tech hub for the performing arts flaunts two large spaces: the 2,700-seat Walt Disney Theater, used for Broadway traveling shows and other theatrical events, and the 300-seat Alexis & Jim Pugh Theater.

The Dr. Phillips Center for the Performing Arts

THRILL RIDES

**1 Rock 'n' Roller Coaster®
Starring Aerosmith**
This ride (*p31: Disney's Hollywood Studios®*) accelerates like a military jet. If that isn't enough to make heads spin, each 24-passenger "stretch limo" has 120 speakers that blare Aerosmith hits at a teeth-rattlingly high volume.

2 Flight of Passage
Discover the beauty and grandeur of the world of Pandora on an exhilarating 3D ride inspired by James Cameron's *Avatar*. Located in Pandora – The World of Avatar (*p32: Disney's Animal Kingdom®*), this breathtaking coaster is a favorite among film fans.

3 Manta®
Headfirst, face-down in a prone position – mimicking the gliding movements of a manta ray – this ride (*p111: SeaWorld® Orlando*) has its riders soar to the sky, then take a dive, twisting and turning at speeds of up to 60 mph (96 km/h).

4 Hollywood Rip Ride Rockit®
The second-tallest (167 ft/ 51 m) and one of the fastest (65 mph/105 km/h) coasters in Orlando, Hollywood Rip Ride Rockit® (*p34; Universal Studios Florida™*) lets you pick a soundtrack before you strap in to a high-tech car. Visitors can buy a recording of the ride to create their own music video later.

5 Splash Mountain®
Prepare to get drenched on this deep-drop ride (*p25: Magic Kingdom®*). In summer, it's a cooling trip; at any time of year, it's one to enjoy as a spectator from the bridge between Frontierland® and Adventureland®. Even in that relative safety you may get soaked.

6 Mako
Named after one of the fastest sharks in the ocean, this wild ride (*p111; SeaWorld® Orlando*) is the fastest (73 mph, 118 km/h), tallest, and longest in Orlando. Putting the hype in this hypercoaster is a feeling of near weightlessness known as "air time," as you speed through the reef, hunting for prey.

7 Incredible Hulk Coaster®
Possibly the ultimate inversion ride, this is a zero-G-force, multi-looping coaster (*p39: Universal's Islands of Adventure™*). The latest enhancements add additional storylines to the ride – as you wait in line, audio-visuals set you in the middle of an experiment gone wrong.

**Hollywood Rip Ride
Rockit® coaster**

Striking facade of the Twilight Zone Tower of Terror™

8 Twilight Zone Tower of Terror™

Take the plunge on the phantom elevator that crosses into the Twilight Zone (p31: Disney's Hollywood Studios®) at the Hollywood Tower Hotel. According to legend, in 1939 five elevator passengers disappeared during a violent thunderstorm, never to be seen again. Not suitable for young children.

9 Kraken®

Think pure speed as Poseidon's mythological underwater beast breaks free and pulls your 32-passenger train 151 ft (46 m) closer to the sky without warning, then dives 144 ft (44 m) back toward the ground at speeds of 65 mph (105 km/h). After this descent, expect seven loops on a 4,177-ft (1,273-m) course (p111: SeaWorld® Orlando). This may just be the longest 3 minutes and 39 seconds of your life.

10 Summit Plummet

No water-park slide will get your heart pumping faster than this 120-ft (36-m) partial-darkness ride at Blizzard Beach (p101). It starts slow, but ends in a near vertical drop that has you plummeting at a breakneck speed of 60 mph (96 km/h). It's not for the weak of heart or those under 48 inches (122 cm).

TOP 10 GENTLER RIDES

1. The Cat in the Hat™
This ride's (p39) dizzying, 24-ft (7-m) tunnel can put your tummy in a spin.

2. Barnstormer
⑨ V1 ⬛ Magic Kingdom®
This circus-stunt-plane coaster spins its way around the whimsical track. It has a minimum height restriction of 35 inches (89 cm).

3. Dumbo
⑨ V1 ⬛ Magic Kingdom®
Fly round and round, while dipping up and down on this tot-friendly ride.

4. The Magic Carpets of Aladdin
⑨ V1 ⬛ Magic Kingdom®
A gentle ride aboard a flying carpet.

5. Flight of the Hippogriff™
Like the Barnstormer and Woody's Nuthouse, the corkscrew action of this ride (p42) is a blast.

6. Pteranodon Flyers®
A neat aerial adventure (p38), but it can make some riders queasy.

7. Peter Pan's Flight
Fly over London and on to Never Land (p22) with Peter and the Lost Boys.

8. Caro-Seuss-el™
Seussian characters make this carousel ride (p40) truly unique.

9. E.T. Adventure®
Pedal your bicycle past fantastic scenery and characters (p34).

10. Woody Woodpecker's Nuthouse Coaster®
The banked turns of this mini coaster at Universal Studios Florida™ (p34) are absolutely exhilarating.

The Cat in the Hat™

SMALLER ATTRACTIONS

1 Winter Park Scenic Boat Tour

Glide through three of Winter Park's lakes on a pontoon boat during this hour-long tour *(p132)*. Spot ospreys and herons, or swoon over huge lake-side mansions. The architecture and calm, secluded canals make this tour popular with the kitsch-weary.

2 Ripley's Believe It or Not!® Odditorium

Ripley's *(p111)* quirky exterior looks like it's about to slip into the ground. Inside you'll find squeal-inducing replicas of human and animal oddities, including a two-headed cat. A movie also shows people swallowing coat hangers and light bulbs, while displays include a *Mona Lisa* made out of toast.

3 Orlando Watersports Complex

🏠 E5 🏠 8615 Florida Roch Rd
Ⓦ ahtionparhs.com ☑

The complex offers outdoor wake boarding, wake skating, wake surfing, and water skiing sessions. Children can splash around at Aquapark, which has slides, climbing towers, and more.

Superb ICON Orlando 360™ observation wheel

4 ICON Orlando 360™

At 400 ft (122 m), this observation wheel *(p112)* at ICON Park Orlando is one of the world's tallest. Passengers get a bird's-eye view of the city, which is an impressive sight by day, and even more so by night. Other entertainment options include the popular Madame Tussauds, SKELETONS: Museum of Osteology, and the Orlando StarFlyer, the world's tallest swing ride at 450 ft (137 m). The complex offers more than a dozen restaurants, and bars. There is a central courtyard with choreographed water displays as well as live entertainment, and unique shopping venues. I-Drive itself is laden with small attractions from one end to the other.

5 iFLY Orlando

Experience skydiving without jumping from a plane at this vertical wind tunnel *(p112)*, which has more than 100,000 visitors each year. There are certain weight restrictions and a minimum age of three, but no experience is necessary. The price covers a class, gear, and equipment, and two 1-minute jumps, usually more than enough to exhaust a novice skydiver.

Boat tour on the lake at Winter Park

6 WonderWorks

Gimmicks abound inside this building *(p110)*, which is designed to appear as if it is sinking into the ground roof-first. Inside, there is an interactive arcade of some mild scientific educational value. Among more than 85 hands-on activities, the curious can experience an earthquake or virtual hang gliding. For more action, try the huge laser-tag field.

7 Orlando Tree Trek Adventure Park

Fly over untouched Floridian wilderness on zip lines and Tarzan swings, choosing from a range of day or night excursions *(p117)*. Courses are available for all skill levels.

8 Nona Adventure Park

F6 14086 Centerline Dr 10am–8pm daily nonaadventurepark.com

This family-focused adventure park features outdoor climbing walls, obstacle courses, and a water park filled with giant inflatables. The Wake Nona offers a state-of-the-art wakeboarding experience.

9 Fun Spot America

Fun Spot's *(p111)* thrilling go-kart tracks and Ferris wheel come with two giant roller coasters and the world's biggest SkyCoaster. For less adventurous visitors, there are also sedate arcade games and a kid zone.

10 Titanic: The Artifact Exhibition

Fans of James Cameron's film will love this impressive, 20,000-sq-ft (1,858 sq-m) re-creation *(p109)* of the doomed *Titanic*, which features 17 galleries filled with artifacts recovered from the wreckage. Guided tours by actors playing passengers and crew bring the displays to life. There's also an interactive dinner event on Friday and Saturday evenings.

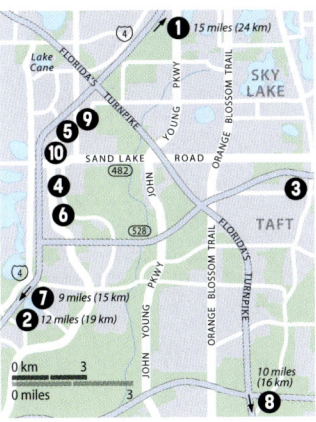

The intriguing upside-down WonderWorks building

PARKS AND PRESERVES

1 Harry P. Leu Gardens
Wander through sprawling 50-acre (20-ha) botanical gardens *(p124)*, best seen from October through March. The stunning flora at the formal gardens includes camellias, orchids, azaleas, and 75 varieties of roses. There are gardens devoted to palms, bamboo, and butterflies, too.

2 Canaveral National Seashore
◙ X5 ◙ Titusville ◙ 6am–6pm daily
◙ nps.gov/cana ◙◙
The scenic federal preserves of Canaveral National Seashore and Merritt Island National Wildlife Refuge *(p48)*, bordering the Kennedy Space Center, are home to endangered sea turtles, manatees, dolphins, alligators, bald eagles, and ospreys. Explore Canaveral's beaches and Merritt's driving routes, trails, and observation deck.

3 Lake Eola Park
Enjoy a leisurely stroll along the 0.9-mile (1.4-km) trail that circles the lake here *(p123)*. Less energetic pursuits include feeding the birds and cruising Lake Eola in the swan-shaped rental boats. The park also hosts seasonal events, including a 4th of July fireworks show. Orlando's farmers' market is held here on Sundays.

4 Bill Frederick Park at Turkey Lake
◙ D3 ◙ 3401 S. Hiawassee Rd
◙ Apr–Oct: 8am–7pm daily; Nov–Mar: 8am–5pm daily
◙ orlando.gov ◙
Unlike many more spartan state parks, this 300-acre (121-ha) city retreat has a swimming pool, picnic pavilions, a lake full of fish, nature and jogging trails, three playgrounds, and canoes and kayaks for rent. It also has camping areas.

5 Lake Louisa State Park
◙ W5 ◙ State Park Dr, Clermont
◙ 8am–sunset daily ◙ floridastate parks.org ◙
At this state park, visitors can fish, swim, or paddle a canoe, but you'll have to bring your own equipment. The beach has a bathhouse with showers, and there's a picnic area. White-tail deer, wild turkeys, marsh rabbits, opossums, and raccoons are common, and a polecat may cut across your path.

Exploring the serene
Harry P. Leu Gardens

6 Disney Wilderness Preserve

⊞ B2 **⌂** 2700 Scrub Jay Trail,
Kissimmee **⊙** 9am–4:30pm
Mon–Fri **⊠** nature.org

The centerpiece of the Everglades
Headwaters National Wildlife Refuge
and Conservation Center, this preserve
is a center for research on climate
change. It is also a great place to hike
as it hosts over 1,000 species of flora
and fauna – look out for bald eagles,
wood storks, sandhill cranes, gopher
tortoises, and big-eared bats among
the cypress swamps, oak hammocks,
and freshwater marshes.

7 Lake Apopka Wildlife Drive

B3 **⌂** 2803 Lust Rd, Apopha
⊙ Sunrise–sunset Fri–Sun
⊠ lakeapophawildlife.us

This lovely birding and wildlife drive
is just an 11-mile (18-km) trip around
the north shore of the fourth-largest
lake in Florida. Visitors can see nearly
200 species of birds, turtles, bobcats,
otters, raccoons, alligators, snakes,
and coyotes.

8 Blue Spring State Park

With the largest natural spring on
the St. Johns River, pouring out nearly
100 million gallons (450 million liters) of
water a day, Blue Spring State Park

(p95) is a winter refuge for manatees.
Swimmers and snorkelers alike will
enjoy the refreshing waters. Fishing,
canoeing, and boating are popular
activities here.

9 Wekiwa Springs State Park

⊞ A3 **⌂** 1800 Wekiwa Circle, Apopha
⊙ 8am–sunset daily **⊠** floridastate
parks.org ⊿

These springs provide a fertile habitat
for such species as white-tail deer,
gray foxes, bobcats, raccoons, and
black bears. They also provide some
of the best places for paddling in a
boat in Central Florida. Canoe rentals
and picnic and camping areas are
also available.

10 Tosohatchee Wildlife Management Area

⊞ W5 **⌂** Christmas, 18 miles (29 km)
E of Orlando **⊙** 8am–sunset daily
⊠ myfwc.com ⊿

Swamps dotted with hardwood
hammocks (islands covered in
shady tropical forest) and a 19-mile
(30-km) stretch of the St. Johns
River combine to make this one of
Central Florida's prettiest, unspoiled
parks. Look out for wild orchids and
other flora. Hawks, eagles, and fox
squirrels can be seen from the trails
and alligator, otter, and turtles are
found in the water.

Tubing in the Blue Spring State Park

Clockwise from above
**Sunset at Lake
Apopka; two
blue-winged teals
swimming on the
lake; a baby
alligator spotted
in the area**

PLACES TO COOL OFF

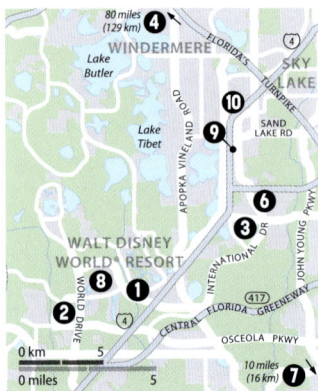

offers the features and personalized services of an upscale island resort. Admission is not cheap, but includes everything from lunch to wet suits and sun block. It gets booked up fast so reserve your ticket at least two months in advance.

1 Typhoon Lagoon

This Disney water park (p101) is an enthralling mix of slides, tubes, and the largest wave pool in the U.S. It's suited to families with pre-teen children who'll appreciate the gentler nature of the attractions. One stand-out is Humunga Kowabanga, where visitors shoot down a near-vertical five-story drop. Visitors can pay an extra fee for surfing lessons at the wave pool outside of regular opening hours.

2 Blizzard Beach

Currently claiming the top spot among Orlando's water parks, Blizzard Beach (p101) has a uniquely themed twist: it's what a ski resort would be like if it started to melt, with waterslides replacing ski runs. With seven waterslides and some excellent rides, a wave pool, and kids' areas, it can reach capacity early and close to new admissions until later in the day.

3 Discovery Cove®

Want to unwind on a tropical beach or snorkel near coral reefs? This exclusive (daily entry is limited to 1,000 people) attraction (p109)

4 Fun2Dive Scuba, Snorkeling, and Manatee Tours

V4 **2880 Seabreeze Point, Crystal River** **fun2dive.com**
Watch extraordinary manatees from the boat, or float from a safe distance so as not to disturb them on these full-day tours. Sessions run year-round, but the best time to go is migration season from November through March. Groups are kept to six or under, and drinks, snorkeling gear, and sunscreen are provided. Best for ages 5 and above.

5 Orlando's Natural Springs

Orlando may be better known for its not-so-natural attractions, but it does have some beautiful unspoiled scenery. As well as Wekiwa Springs (p67) and Blue Spring State Park (p95), there's DeLeon Springs State Park, Alexander and Juniper Springs, and Silver Springs State Park. All offer a variety of activities, such as snorkeling, paddleboat rentals, fishing, hiking, and kayaking.

A glass-bottom boat in Silver Springs State Park

Thrill rides at the Aquatica® water park in SeaWorld®

6 Aquatica®

This unique water park *(p110)* at SeaWorld® allows you to swim through sealife in a high-speed tube slide. Half-pipes and giant wave pools also keep you entertained. Popular rides include Ihu's Breakaway Falls®, a tower slide that sends riders on a 40-ft (12-m) vertical drop before being swept into a steep waterslide, and Taumata Racer®, a thrilling mat ride.

7 Lakefront Park

This family-oriented park *(p119)* includes a marina, a children's play-ground, picnic areas with grills, a performing arts pavilion, walking and biking trails, a white-sand beach, volleyball courts, and a water fountain playground with a great view of pic-turesque East Lake Tohopekaliga.

8 Splash Pads at Disney's EPCOT®

📍 W2 🏠 1200 EPCOT® Resort Blvd 🌐 disneyworld.com 🔗

Splash pads are integrated into several attractions throughout Walt Disney World®, but these ones, near Mission Space and Test Track, are there for no other reason than to help hot and tired visitors of all ages cool off. Dancing water fountains and bubbling water provide relief from the heat and humidity.

9 CoCo Key Water Resort

📍 T3 🕐 Winter: 11am–5pm daily; summer: 11am–9pm daily 🌐 cocokeyorlando.com 🔗

With 14 slides and three heated pools, the outdoor water park here is perfect for splashing around all day. In addition, the resort is home to three restaurants and an arcade. Tickets for the water park are sold separately.

10 Universal's Volcano Bay™

📍 T2 🏠 Adventure Way 🕐 Hours vary, check website 🌐 universalorlando.com

This astonishing volcanic island-themed park will satisfy thrill-seekers with its intense body slides and high-speed rides, but there are plenty of calmer attractions, including winding rivers, sandy beaches, and several play areas. Resort-style facilities are located throughout the park.

SPAS

1 Mandara Spa at the Loews Portofino Bay Hotel

T1 5601 Universal Blvd 10am–6pm daily loewshotels.com

A variety of indulgent massages, facials, and body treatments await visitors at this Balinese-inspired spa. Guests of the hotel can arrange in-room massages. A sauna, full-service salon, and a fitness center round out the offerings.

2 Senses Spa at Disney's Grand Floridian Resort & Spa

V1 4401 Floridian Way 9am–6pm daily disneyworld.disney.go.com

This spa at Disney's Victorian-style resort offers water and massage therapies, aromatherapy, body wraps, and masks. Special services for kids aged 4 to 12 are also available.

3 Spa at the Four Seasons Resort Orlando

W1 10100 Dream Tree Blvd, Lake Buena Vista 9am–8pm daily fourseasons.com/orlando/spa

A serene oasis where guests can refresh body, mind, and spirit through an array of treatments, from touch therapy to body polishes, and facials. Kids can be transformed into royal princesses and knights with makeup, costumes, and hairstyling.

4 Relâche Spa at the Gaylord Palms

X3 6000 W. Osceola Pkwy, Kissimmee 9am–5pm daily marriott.com

This full-service spa offers an array of relaxing treatments including aromatherapy massage, organic facial treatments tailored to your skin's needs, moisturizing manicures, and exfoliating pedicures. Hairstyling and salon services are also offered.

5 Mandara Spa at Walt Disney World Swan and Dolphin Resort

W2 1500 EPCOT® Resorts Blvd, Buena Vista 9am–5pm Mon–Wed, 8am–8pm Thu–Sun mandaraspa.com

Relax at this Balinese-themed full-service spa before or after treatments in the Meditation or Tea Gardens. Signature treatments include a

The spa at the Four Seasons Resort

Relaxing session at the Mandara Spa

coconut poultice massage or a Florida orange blossom body scrub, exclusive to this location.

6 Mokara Spa at the Omni Orlando Resort

H1 **1500 Masters Blvd, Championsgate** **9am–5pm Mon–Fri, 9am–6pm Sat, 10am–5pm Sun** **mokaraspas.com/orlando**

This first-class spa provides state-of-the-art treatments and a deluxe fitness facility. From aromatherapy facials to sports massages, clients can take a break from the crowds at this secret resort and have a relaxing spa day.

7 Poseidon Spa at Grand Bohemian

P3 **325 S. Orange Ave** **10am–6pm daily** **grandbohemianhotel.com**

The Grand Bohemian is a landmark luxury hotel, and the Poseidon Spa only adds to its acclaim. This tranquil spa offers several therapeutic treatments and massages, facials, manicures, and pedicures. In-room services are also available.

8 Blue Harmony Spa®

X3 **14651 Chelonia Pkwy** **10am–6pm daily** **wyndhamgrandorlando.com**

This elegantly designed spa is located in the Wyndham Grand Orlando Resort

Bonnet Creek, close to Disney World®. It offers a host of treatments; look out for the weekly specials on signature treatments, with different discounted packages on offer each day of the week.

9 The Waldorf Astoria Spa

X3 **14200 Bonnet Creek Resort Ln** **9am–5pm Sun–Thu, 9am–8pm Fri & Sat** **waldorfastoriaorlando.com**

Unwind in the luxuriously calm, serene atmosphere at The Waldorf Astoria, and enjoy a range of pampering treatments, including body therapies, massages, and facials, as well as a selection of salon services. There's also a steam room and Jacuzzi on site, along with a tea lounge.

10 The Spa at the Ritz-Carlton Grande Lakes

F4 **4012 Central Florida Pkwy** **9am–5pm Mon–Fri, 9am–7pm Sat & Sun** **ritzcarlton.com/en/Properties/Orlando/Spa**

A day in this spa is time well spent. Start with a facial in one of the spa's 40 treatment rooms; go for a swim in the private 4,000-sq-ft (375-sq-m) outdoor lap pool; or enjoy a rejuvenating massage followed by a visit to the boutique. End your outing with a lovely dinner at the spa's popular restaurant.

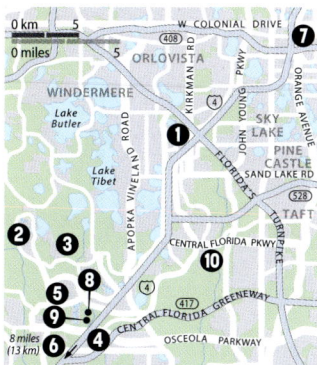

SPORTS AND OUTDOOR ACTIVITIES

1 ESPN Wide World of Sports Complex

📍 W3 🏠 Walt Disney World®
🕐 Hours vary, chech website
🌐 espnwwos.com 🔗

Watch events or participate in 60 sports at this vast facility, with ten world-class fields, courts, and arenas. ESPN Wide World of Sports merchandise is also available here.

2 Tennis

There are some great clay courts at Disney's Grand Floridian Resort & Spa (disneyworld.disney.go.com), Saratoga Springs Resort & Spa, Disney's Bay Lake Tower, BoardWalk Inn & Villas, Old Key West, and The Swan & Dolphin. Beyond Disney, the nearby Grand Cypress Racquet Club (ustaflorida.com) has 12 excellent tennis courts.

3 Horseback Riding

Tri-Circle-D Ranch at Disney's popular Fort Wilderness Resort (disneyworld.disney.go.com) offers 45-minute guided trail rides on horseback or in a carriage through the woodlands. Smaller children can take a pony ride.

4 Boating

Many of the lovely artificial lakes around Walt Disney World® (disneyworld.disney.go.com) have small motorboats and pontoon boats for rent. There are also paddleboats for those who prefer more of a workout.

5 Cycling

Get away on Disney's scenic bike trails. You can rent single- and multi-speed bikes, or a Segway® at the Fort Wilderness Resort's Bike Barn (407-824-2932) to explore one of the wilderness trails. Tandems and cycles with baby seats and

**Riding a Segway®,
Fort Wilderness Resort**

Invictus Games, ESPN Wide World of Sports Complex

training wheels are also available. Two-, four-, and six-person Surrey bicycles are also available for rent at a number of Disney locations.

6 Watersports

Winter Park has a number of serene lakes, which are perfect for enjoying paddle boarding. Paddleboard Orlando (paddleboardorlando. com) at Lake Killarney offers classes by qualified instructors.

7 Swimming

Swimmers in Orlando are spoiled for choice with two beautiful sea coasts, springs, and lakes. Hotel pools (p148) range from lazy rivers to quiet spas.

8 Surfing

According to the state's surf enthusiasts, Disney's Typhoon Lagoon (p101) has wave-making down to a fine art. Ron Jon Surf School (ronjonsurfschool.com) on Cocoa Beach holds regular classes for beginners.

9 Fishing

The city offers some high-adrenaline sports fishing out on the ocean, as well as more tranquil days fishing off a pier or jetty. Land your dinner with Pro Bass Guide Service (psbassguidefl.com), a Winter Garden outfit that specializes in guided bass-fishing trips to some of Central Florida's most picturesque rivers and lakes. There are also offshore expeditions for saltwater species.

10 Wagon Rides

Take an old-fashioned wagon ride along the picturesque trails at Fort Wilderness (disney world.disney.go.com). Expect plenty of singing and dancing, and a good-time atmosphere on this 25-minute ride.

TOP 10 SPORTING EVENTS

Florida Citrus Bowl

1. Florida Citrus Bowl
Jan 1
Annual college football showdown between the top teams.

2. Walt Disney World® Marathon
Early Jan W disneyworld.com
Annual 26.2-mile (42-km) race.

3. Bike Weeks
Early Feb
Two weeks of motor action at Daytona Beach, ending with the Daytona 500.

4. Orlando City Soccer
Feb–Aug
Watch professional teams in action.

5. Arnold Palmer Invitational
Mar
A top golf tournament played in memory of golf legend Arnold Palmer.

6. Atlanta Braves Spring Training
Mar W braves.com
Catch baseball team Atlanta Braves in pre-season training.

7. Orlando Pride
Apr–Oct
Watch Orlando's National Women's Soccer League team.

8. Silver Spurs Rodeo
Jun & Oct W silverspurs rodeo.com
These large-scale rodeo events are held twice a year in Kissimmee.

9. Children's Miracle Network Classic
Mid-Oct
Tour pros in a week of golfing events.

10. Orlando Magic
Oct–Apr
Don't miss the NBA team in season.

GOLF COURSES

cypress stands line the fairways; a 5-tee system accommodates all skill levels. (Max yd: 7,108 [6,500 m]. USGA rating: 74.6.)

4 Disney's Palm
📍 V1 🏠 Palm Dr 🌐 disney world.com

This jewel of a course is surrounded by woodlands. Half of its holes have water, and its 94 bunkers create headaches for those whose shots stray. The 18th hole is one of the toughest on the PGA Tour. (Max yd: 6,957 [6,391 m]. USGA rating: 73.) Golf lessons are offered on the course.

5 Villas of Grand Cypress Golf Club
📍 X2 🏠 1 N. Jacaranda 🌐 grand cypress.com

This highly rated 45-hole course was designed by golfer Jack Nicklaus. The New Course was inspired by the Old Course at St. Andrews in Scotland. The club is semi-private with some public tee times. (Max yd: 6,906 [6,315 m]. USGA rating: 74.4.)

1 ChampionsGate
📍 H1 🏠 1400 Masters Blvd 🌐 championsgategolf.com

Greg Norman created two 18-hole courses for this resort southwest of Disney, featuring activities for those who choose not to golf. Between them they have 13 water holes, and share double greens at the 4th and 16th holes. (Max yd: 7,048 [6,445 m] and 7,407 [6,773 m], respectively. USGA rating: 75.1 & 76.3.) There are one-on-one lessons, too.

2 Disney's Lake Buena Vista
📍 X2 🏠 Buena Vista Dr 🌐 disney world.com

This tight course has heavily bunkered fairways, a pine forest, and an unusual island green on the 7th hole. (Max yd: 6,819 [6,325 m]. USGA rating: 72.7.)

3 Waldorf Astoria Golf Club
📍 X3 🏠 14200 Bonnet Creek Resort Ln 🌐 waldorfastoria orlando.com

Rees Jones designed this 18-hole course around the contours of a wetland preserve. Impressive pine and

Golfers at the Villas of Grand Cypress Golf Club

6 Ritz-Carlton Golf Club Grande Lakes

F4 **4040 Central Florida Phwy** **grandelakes.com**

This 18-hole Greg Norman course is certified as an Audubon Cooperative Sanctuary. You can enjoy thriving wetlands and take lessons, while playing on a PGA course. (Max yd: 7,122 [6,512 m]. USGA rating: 73.9.)

7 Arnold Palmer's Bay Hill Club & Lodge

E2 **9000 Bay Hill Rd** **bay hill.com**

Arnold Palmer designed this sweeping course, located along the Butler chain of lakes. Among the oldest courses in the area, it has been redesigned to include two championship courses, a nine-hole challenge course, and the Arnold Palmer Golf Academy. (Max yd: 7,381 [6,749 m]. USGA rating: none.)

8 Disney's Magnolia

V1 **Palm Dr** **disney world.com**

Here's a course with forgivingly wide fairways that let you hammer the ball. But don't get reckless: 11 of the 18 holes contain water and the course has 97 bunkers. Part of the PGA's Funai Golf Classic is played here. (Max yd: 7,190 [6,574 m]. USGA rating: 73.9.)

9 Tranquilo Golf Club at Four Seasons

W1 **Golf View Dr** **four seasons.com**

One of the more challenging 18-hole golf clubs, the Tom Fazio-designed Osprey Ridge features native wood-lands, elevated tees, fairly large greens, nine water holes, and more than 70 bunkers. *Golf Digest's* "Places to Play" ranks it among Florida's best public and resort courses. (Max yd: 7,101 [6,493 m]. USGA rating: 74.4.)

10 Reunion Golf

H1 **7599 Gathering Dr** **reunionresort.com**

Nowhere else will you find three signature courses designed by the likes of Jack Nicklaus, Tom Watson, and Arnold Palmer, all in a single location. Each course offers a unique experience, whether in the form of rolling hills, smooth long fairways, or strategically placed bunkers. (Max yd: 7,244 [6,624m], USGA rating: Palmer 73.4, Watson 74.7, Nicklaus 76.7.)

OFF THE BEATEN PATH

Enjoying a Boggy Creek airboat ride

of his buildings on one site. Some of the highlights include the Annie Pfeiffer Chapel, the Roux Library, the Danforth Chapel, and the Esplanades. Pick up a walking-tour map from the visitor center.

1 Boggy Creek Airboat Adventures

This ride *(p120)*, appropriate for everyone in the family, offers a unique chance to see nature from aboard an airboat. Speeding (and sometimes stopping) through the wetlands and marshes of the headwaters of the Florida Everglades, you'll see turtles, alligators, birds, and more. The best time to see the wildlife is early in the morning (on a hot day) or in the evening (on a cooler day).

2 The Citrus Tower
W5 141 N. Hwy 27, Clermont 9am–5pm Mon–Sat citrus tower.com

Built in 1956 on one of Florida's highest points, this venerable 226-ft- (69-m-) tall observation tower gives a 360-degree view of the rolling hills and hundreds of spring-fed lakes in the eight counties surrounding it. The tip of its highest antenna reaches a height of 500 ft (152 m) above sea level.

3 Florida Southern College
W5 111 Lake Hollingsworth Dr, Lakeland flsouthern.edu

In the late 1930s, architect Frank Lloyd Wright designed 12 campus buildings at this college – the largest collection

4 Safari Wilderness Ranch
Take a tour of animal habitats and learn about Florida's natural history and several conservation programs that have been undertaken at this working game ranch *(p117)*.

5 Lakeridge Winery
W5 19239 U.S.-27, Clermont 10am–5pm Mon–Sat, 11am–5pm Sun lakeridgewinery.com

Winery tours begin with a 15-minute video on the wine-making process in Florida, then you'll get to visit the production area and see the vineyards. Finally, you can taste a fine selection of Lakeridge's award-winning wines. The winery also holds various festivals and music events throughout the year.

6 Central Florida Zoo and Botanical Gardens
W4 3755 N.W. Hwy 17-92, Sanford centralfloridazoo.org

Beneath the zoo's dense canopy of foliage, visitors can observe the residents (from howler monkeys to bald eagles) at close quarters. Some areas are more exciting than others but, on the whole, this makes for a rewarding trip.

7 Eco Tours at the Ritz Carlton and JW Marriott Grande Lakes
F4 4012 Central Florida Pkwy 407-206-2400

A two-hour guided canoe or kayak tour of Shingle Creek, the headwaters to the Florida Everglades, gives guests a taste of old Florida. While paddling, you'll learn the history of Shingle

Creek from your water guides. Be sure to keep an eye out for alligators, bald eagles, osprey, and barred owls. Guided tours are held every day at 9:30am and 1pm.

8 Stetson Mansion

📍 W4 🏠 1031 Camphor La, Deland 🌐 stetsonmansion.com ↗

Take a tour of Florida's most opulent and historic home and estate. Built for hatmaker and philanthropist John B. Stetson, the house has been restored to showcase its unusual blend of cottage, Gothic, Tudor, Moorish, and Polynesian styles. Note, credit cards are not accepted here.

9 St. Johns Rivership Company

📍 W4 🏠 433 N. Palmetto Ave 🌐 stjohnsrivershipco.com ↗

Operating out of historic Sanford, the 1946-built triple-decked *Barbara-Lee* offers daily cruises along the scenic St Johns River. It's a truly civilized way to catch a glimpse of the Florida that tourists rarely see.

10 Crystal River and Homosassa Springs

📍 V4 🏠 River Ventures, 498 S.E. Kings Bay Dr, Crystal River 🌐 riverventures.com ↗

A variety of boats tour year-round on the Crystal River and Homosassa Springs, allowing visitors to swim near manatees. Sightings of these gentle creatures are most frequent from late October to late March.

Kayaking in the waters of the Crystal River

LIVE MUSIC VENUES

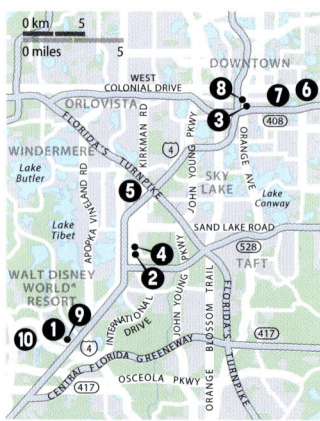

1 House of Blues® Restaurant & Bar

This huge venue *(p103)* is a go-to for music fans in the area. House of Blues® books amazing acts in every genre, from hip-hop to death metal. Shows here start and end on time, the sound system is crystal clear, and the decor is suitably funky. Perhaps the one flaw is a lack of any seating with a stage view, so be prepared to be on your feet all night.

2 Blue Martini

📍 T3 🏠 9101 International Dr 🌐 orlando.bluemartini.com

Serving up 42 signature martinis and specialty cocktails of every flavor and color, this vibrant spot – with live music nightly – is popular with young professionals, in part thanks to a post-work happy hour for sharing plates; a light menu is also on offer. The outdoor patio bar is a good place to mingle.

3 Bösendorfer Lounge

The lounge music obsession that once swept the nation is now only for serious practitioners. This elegant hotel bar *(p126)* is the perfect place to sip cocktails and admire the performers in evening dress, who sing near the $250,000 Bösendorfer Grand piano.

4 Howl at the Moon

Dance till you drop at this lively I-Drive location that's part bar, part concert venue *(p114)*. Bands belt out favorites from the 1980s and 1990s, along with today's top party hits. The drinks menu is extensive, including a slew of signature cocktails.

5 Hard Rock Live

📍 T1 🏠 6050 Universal Blvd, CityWalk™ 🌐 hardrock.com/live/locations/orlando

Hard Rock offers a comfortable setting for concerts, with balcony seating and good stage views. Dubbed "the Coliseum of Rock" due to its impressive entrance, imposing columns, and grand archways, this venue welcomes top artists like Maxwell and Erykah Badu, who play to large crowds.

6 The Plaza Live

📍 P4 🏠 425 N. Bumby Ave 🌐 plazaliveorlando.org

Originally the city's first two-screen movie house, this is Orlando's premier concert venue, hosting bands, comedians, and cultural events. There's a seated balcony and standing space.

7 Tin Roof

📍 T3 🏠 8371 International Dr 🌐 tinrooforlando.com

Making a great addition to the lively ICON Park Orlando™ (home of the ICON Orlando 360™; *p112*), the Tin Roof has a vintage 1950s vibe, and serves up lunch and dinner along with nightly live entertainment. Performances come from both famous and not-so-famous acts, ensuring that the entertainment here is an ever-changing affair.

Live music at the legendary Social club

8 The Social

This Downtown club (*p126*) offers an eclectic mix of live music from both established acts and up-and-coming artists. For years, the club's policy of booking top national touring acts meant it was the shining light of Orlando's live music scene. Now competition from larger clubs is stiffer, but this spot, with its stylishly raw decor, remains O-Town's favorite venue to enjoy live music.

9 Raglan Road

📍 X2 🏠 Disney Springs™ 🌐 raglanroad.com

Named after a street in Dublin, this welcoming pub offers Irish music and lively foot-stomping dance performances. You can stay inside the Victorian-style pub or take a seat on the outdoor terrace while enjoying a vast menu of tasty dishes, ranging from fish and chips to gourmet Irish burgers.

10 Atlantic Dance Hall

📍 W2 🏠 Disney's BoardWalk 🕐 Sun & Mon 🌐 disneyworld.disney.go.com 📍

Travel back in time to dance at the glamorous dance halls of the 1930s and '40s. Atlantic Dance Hall features wonderful Art Deco interiors and is ideally located for those staying at a Disney resort. Note that this venue is for ages 21 and above.

Bar area at the popular Howl at the Moon

FAVORITE LGBTQ+ SPOTS

1 Hamburger Mary's
T3 **110 W. Church St**
hamburgermarys.com/orlando

Tasty appetizers, juicy burgers, and delicious desserts are on the menu, but it's the evening entertainment you'll want to stick around for. Think dining with divas, and you'll soon get the picture. Shows, ranging from an interactive drag show and cabaret to a night of trivia, start at 7 or 7:30pm, with a Broadway Brunch on Sundays.

2 Bösendorfer Lounge
Signature cocktails mixed with soulful jazz draw an upscale crowd to this hotel haunt *(p126)*. Maybe it's the heavy drapes, the dark wood, or the well-tuned ennui of some patrons, but you feel glamorous just being here. It's very popular on Friday and Saturday nights, when you will be treated to live performances – whether it's the tinkling of piano keys or hits sung by jazz and soul groups.

3 District Dive
P3 **2401 E. South St**
407-601-2813

Popular with locals, this hip industrial-looking dive bar is loved for its live music and fun themed nights. Enjoy the casual vibe and order some drinks while chatting with the friendly regulars.

4 Southern Nights
P4 **375 S. Bumby Ave**
407-412-5039

Southern Nights is a mega-club with several bars and performance spaces to choose from. It hosts regular theme nights and fancy-dress evenings, and is famed for its elaborate drag shows and lively diva-hosted dance parties. There's also an outdoor patio for unwinding and relaxing, and a games room with pool tables, darts, and video games. Happy hour is 4pm to 9pm every Wednesday.

Swanky bar area at the Bösendorfer Lounge

Relaxed interior at Mango's
Tropical Cafe

5 Mango's Tropical Cafe
Enjoy an expansive 55,000 sq ft (5,110 sq m) of high-energy glamor, lights, live music, and dancing at Mango's *(p114)*. The Latin Connection Band plays for the dancers on the main stage. However, the main attraction is the dinner and show that features Michael Jackson and Celia Cruz impersonations. Visitors can take salsa lessons and join the nightly Conga Line.

6 The Dust
P3 431 E. Central Blvd
stardustorlando.com

Formerly The Stardust, this spot is a fabulously retro lounge. Expect everything from live music to bingo nights to its famous burlesque shows. There's also a classic tiki bar upstairs.

7 BarCodes
L1 4453 Edgewater Dr
407-412-6917

Located north of the city, this fun nightspot attracts a more mature clientele than the 20-something crowds elsewhere. As it's just down the road from Hank's, don't be surprised to see patrons bouncing between both bars on any given evening. There's leather night the last Saturday of every month, karaoke on Mondays, and underwear parties Wednesday and Sunday.

8 Savoy Orlando
P3 1913 N. Orange Ave
savoyorlando.com

A sophisticated North Orange lounge that caters for an upscale crowd of mostly professional gay men. High bar tables, black leather stools, and crystal chandeliers give the club a classy air.

9 Renaissance Theater Company
M3 415 E. Princeton St
rentheatre.com

Watch fun-filled drag shows and experimental fringe theater in this warehouse space.

10 Hank's
L1 5026 Edgewater Dr
hanksbarorlando.com

Hank's has been open for over 20 years and is one of Orlando's oldest gay bars. Pool tables, darts, video games, and a jukebox make this unpretentious beer and wine bar a casual hangout. The Back Room, the adjoining adult store, is open nightly.

50's Prime Time Café at Disney's Hollywood Studios®

DINING EXPERIENCES

1 Sleuths Mystery Dinner Shows
📍 T3 🏠 8267 International Dr
🕐 Show times vary 🌐 sleuths.com
This mystery extravaganza features twelve different shows staged in three theaters over the course of a month, each with a suspicious death, and a twist before the mystery is finally uncovered. The dinner includes hors d'oeuvres before the show, then your choice of mains, plus side dishes, dessert, and unlimited beer, wine, and sodas. In addition to the regular dinner show, Sleuths also offers select after-hours productions – mainly comedy shows – aimed at an adult audience.

2 Rainforest Café
Huge model animals and birds provide good company at this beloved rainforest-themed café (p105) in Disney's Animal Kingdom® Park. Expect tasty American-style food and a soundtrack of thunder claps and rainstorms.

3 50's Prime Time Café
Home-cooked-style comfort foods, from pot roast to meatloaf, are all on the menu here (p105) – and portions are generous. Vintage TV sets showing reruns of I Love Lucy add to the 1950s vibe in one of Disney's Hollywood Studios® most popular dining spots. If you want a table, reserve in advance.

4 The Outta Control Magic Comedy Dinner Show
📍 T4 🏠 WonderWorks, 9067 International Dr 🕐 6pm & 8pm daily 🌐 wonderworksonline.com
The audience becomes a part of the show in Tony Brent's 90-minute interactive mixture of magic and fast-paced improvisational comedy. Impersonations and mind-reading are accompanied by delicious pizza, salad, beer, and soda. For all ages.

5 T-REX™
A paradise for pint-sized paleontologists, this restaurant (p104) has dense prehistoric plant life everywhere you turn, along with bubbling geysers, meteor showers, and an endless number of prehistoric special effects (including very life-like animatronic dinosaurs).

6 Sci-Fi Dine-in Theater Restaurant
Step back in time and into your car at this popular restaurant (p105) featuring a very convincing drive-in movie

theme, complete with B-movies playing on the big screen under a starlit sky. Food is secondary to the atmosphere, but the sandwiches and burgers will surely fill you up. Advance reservations are advised.

7 Hoop-Dee-Doo Musical Revue

Reserve well in advance for this show (p103), Disney's most popular "chow-and-cheer" night, at the Fort Wilderness Resort. The jokes are silly, the stars dress in costumes from Broadway's *Oklahoma!*, and if you don't join in the singalong fun, the actors and audience will keep on at you until you do. Dinner is all-you-care-to-enjoy fried chicken, barbecue ribs, and tossed green salad. There's also a vegetarian menu, available with 24 hours' notice.

8 Boma – Flavors of Africa

This African-themed restaurant (p105) is located in Disney's Animal Kingdom Lodge. Dishes from more than 50 countries in the continent are served from the open kitchen for breakfast and dinner. There's a good selection of grilled meats, salads, and pastries. The dinner buffet also offers family-friendly options.

9 Café Tu Tu Tango

The menu here (p115) is described as Spanish tapas but the food is international in flavor, with such diverse nibbles as baked goat's cheese, tuna sashimi, alligator bites, and snapper fingers. Performers (from sword eaters to artists at work) provide the entertainment. Craft cocktails are on offer, too.

10 'Ohana

Flavorful meals such as spicy peel-n-eat shrimp, delicious grilled chicken, and 'Ohana Noodles are on offer at this Polynesian-themed diner (p104). Entertainment is subject to change, but storytelling and hula dancing are often on the agenda.

TOP 10
DINE-OUTS WITH DISNEY AND UNIVERSAL CHARACTERS

1. Cinderella's Royal Table
A whole host of Disney characters join you for this one-of-a-kind dining experience (p105) in the Cinderella Castle at the Magic Kingdom®.

2. Akershus Royal Banquet Hall
Dine on authentic Norwegian fare alongside Disney princesses at EPCOT®.

3. Tusker House Restaurant
Dressed in safari garb, Donald Duck and friends join guests at this African-inspired restaurant in Disney's Animal Kingdom® Park.

4. 1900 Park Fare
Have breakfast with beloved characters such as Mary Poppins or a sit-down dinner with other Disney favorites at the Grand Floridian Resort.

5. Hollywood & Vine
You'll be joined by characters from the Disney Junior TV network at breakfast and lunch. Minnie and friends sometimes pop in for dinner.

6. Chef Mickey's
Mickey hosts American buffet breakfasts and dinners in Disney's Contemporary Resort.

7. Garden Grill Restaurant
This slowly revolving restaurant boasts a feast of farm-fresh foods and mealtime visits from Chip 'n' Dale.

8. The Crystal Palace
Meet Pooh and his pals for buffet breakfasts, lunches, and dinners in the Magic Kingdom®.

9. Topolino's Terrace
Mickey and friends pop in for breakfast at this rooftop restaurant in Disney's Riviera Resort.

10. Cape May Café
Join Goofy for an all-you-care-to-enjoy breakfast buffet at the Beach Club Resort.

PLACES TO SHOP

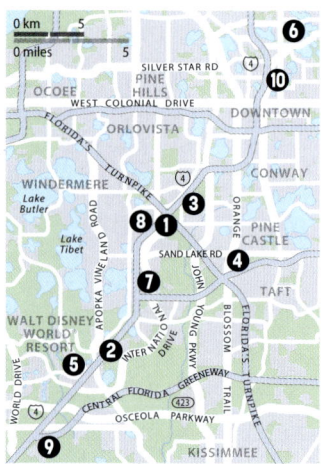

2 Orlando Vineland Premium Outlets

F3 8200 Vineland Ave
premiumoutlets.com

Located just across I-4 from the east entrance of Disney World®, this terrific 150-store complex has it all. Take your pick from an array of options that include posh designer outlets from Versace, DKNY, and Barney's New York, as well as a mix of popular brands, such as Nike, Timberland, and Banana Republic.

3 Mall at Millenia

E4 4200 Conroy Rd
mallatmillenia.com

Upscale and uptown, the Mall at Millenia is home to luxury retailers including Tiffany & Co., Louis Vuitton, Neiman Marcus, and Jimmy Choo, as well as mid-price stores like Macy's, Pottery Barn, and Gap. Valet parking and currency exchange are available, and there's also a U.S. Post Office in the mall, which is very convenient for mailing purchases home or sending gifts. Special events held here include fashion expos and interactive children's activities. Central Florida's only IKEA store is also right across the road from here.

1 Orlando International Premium Outlets

U1 4951 International Dr
premiumoutlets.com

Featuring over 180 stores and offering a wide range of products, this mall houses high-end outlet stores such as Perry Ellis, Michael Kors, Lacoste, Coach, Kate Spade, Aeropostale, The Diamond Co., Movado, Bose, Victoria's Secret, Adidas, and Le Creuset.

Shoppers at the Mall at Millenia

4 Florida Mall
E4 ◻ 8001 S. Orange Blossom
Trail W simon.com
Hugely popular with visitors and
locals, this is one of the best suburban
malls in Central Florida. Stores include
Armani Exchange, Vera Bradley, Coach,
M&M's World, and more than 200 others.

5 Disney Springs™
Inspired by real Florida riverside
towns, Disney's waterside shopping,
entertainment, and dining district
(p99) offers a fantastic range of Disney-
themed stores, stylish boutiques, and
souvenir kiosks. Town Center offers
high-end shopping, with boutiques
including Kate Spade, Coach, Free
People, Lucky Brand, and Lacoste,
among others. West Side, in addition
to its restaurants and entertainment
venues, also adds a few shops to
the mix.

6 Park Avenue
This eight-block stretch of downtown Winter Park (p131) retains an old-
time feel. Many of the stores on this
lovely avenue are independents, along
with some national chains like Williams
& Sonoma and Lilly Pulitzer. There's no
food court, but the sidewalks are lined
with places for lunch or dinner.

7 Pointe Orlando
T4 ◻ 9101 International Dr
W pointeorlando.com
A shopping, dining, and entertainment
complex with something for every-
one – a 20-plus-screen cinema, a
WonderWorks entertainment center,
BB King's Blues Club and much more.
There are also a number of fine-dining
establishments, more than 20 retail
stores, and lots of specialty ones.

8 Universal CityWalk™
T1 ◻ Universal Orlando
Resort™ W universalorlando.com
Known for its clubs, restaurants, and
entertainment venues, CityWalk™ also
has a number of upscale shops and

Stores and restaurants at
Universal CityWalk™

boutiques. Browse casual resort wear
at The Island Clothing Store, the latest
in skate and surf wear at Quiet Flight
Surf Shop, bright cotton clothing and
accessories at Fresh Produce, and
leather goods and jewelry at Fossil.

9 Celebration
This Disney-designed town and
planned community (p116), across I-4
to the southeast of Walt Disney World®,
features a quaint little downtown
district. Here a number of quality
restaurants, a movie theater, a high-
end hotel, and several small, one-of-
a-kind shops and boutiques can be
found lining Market Street.

10 Ivanhoe Row
N3 ◻ N. Orange Ave
The stretch of antique shops comprising
Ivanhoe Row has thinned out in recent
times due to rising rents, but there are
still more than a dozen stores offering
vintage linens, clothing, jewelry, and
various collectibles. Imported furniture
from Bali and vintage LPs can also be
found here.

ORLANDO FOR FREE

1 Lake Eola Park
This Downtown park *(p123)* features a beautiful lake and monthly farmers' markets, plus free concerts and outdoor theatrical productions in the warmer months.

2 Disney Springs™
Explore this redesigned area, divided into the Landing, the Marketplace, West Side, and Town Center. Filled with shops, restaurants, entertainment venues, and smaller attractions, Disney Springs™ *(p99)* is a hub of activity both day and night. Free concerts are staged at various times.

3 Harry P. Leu Gardens
Visitors can explore the beautiful and extensive gardens *(p124)* at the Harry P. Leu Estate for free on the first Monday of select months.

4 Universal CityWalk™
Acting as the entry point for Universal's theme parks, CityWalk™ *(p87)* is filled with shops, restaurants, and entertainment venues. Free concerts, street performances, and live tapings of a popular TV talk show are held here. You can also ride the water taxis to the Universal resorts for free.

5 Music at Harbor Piazza, Loews Portofino Bay Hotel
"Musica della Notte" (Music of the Night) takes place every evening at Loews Portofino Bay Hotel's *(p72)* Harbor Piazza. This celebration captures the romance of Italy, showcasing classic opera and, on occasion, *popera* (a combination of pop and opera). Special themed nights include Romantico Night, Classico Night, and Italian Festival Night. Performances usually begin at sunset, if weather permits.

6 University of Central Florida Arboretum
🏠 4000 Central Florida Blvd 🕐 9am–4pm daily 🌐 arboretum.ucf.edu
This arboretum has a maze of hiking trails through many ecological habitats, including a magnificent

Pretty monarch butterfly, Harry P. Leu Gardens

**Ornate Chinese pagoda
on Lake Eola Park**

cypress dome, an oak hammock,
and 32 acres (130,000 sq m) of pine
flatwoods. Informative signage
helps you identify various species.

7 Disney's BoardWalk
While the daytime is quiet, the
night brings out carnival games and
street performers. Other than activities
along the BoardWalk (p99) itself, you'll
have a great view of the evening
fireworks display at EPCOT®.

8 Kraft Azalea Gardens
📍 K4 🏠 1364 Alabama Dr ⏰ 8am–
sunset daily 🌐 cityofwinterpark.org
Located on the shore of Lake Maitland,
this 5-acre (20,200-sq-m) garden has
huge Cypress trees and bright azaleas.

9 Grand Bohemian Gallery
A visit to this gallery (p59) lets
you enjoy Orlando's cultural side.

10 Fort Christmas Historical Park
🏠 1300 N. Fort Christmas Rd ⏰ Winter:
8am–6pm daily; summer: 8am–8pm
daily 🌐 orangecountyfl.net
Built on Christmas Day, 1837, during
the Second Seminole War, Fort
Christmas has been re-created in this
historical park. Guests can also visit
Florida Cracker houses, a school,
a sugar cane mill, and a museum.

**Entrance to the Fort Christmas
Historical Park**

TOP 10
BUDGET TIPS

I-Ride Trolley

1. To travel up and down International
Drive, take the I-Ride Trolley, which
stops all along the bustling street, for
just $2 per ride, or $6 for a day pass.

2. If you're not hungry enough for
a full meal, order off the appetizer
menu instead – portions in the
theme parks are large.

3. Take advantage of the free
transportation systems at Disney and
Universal resorts. The schedules (p141)
are worth getting to grips with.

4. Eat your main meal at lunchtime
or earlier than the usual dining times,
when prices are often lower.

5. Purchase Universal® Orlando
theme park tickets ahead of time
online. This can often save you 10
percent, and sometimes even 20
percent, on gate prices.

6. Purchase multi-day theme park
tickets, which are better value the
longer you stay.

7. Watch for discounted room rates,
free dining plans, and other promo-
tional offers throughout the year.

8. Purchase the Disney Dining
Plan (available to Disney resort
guests), which works out much
cheaper than purchasing all the
equivalent meals separately.

9. Bring bottled water to the parks
and refill them at the water fountains.
Parks charge high prices for water,
and it can add up to a big expense.

10. To get to Disney resorts, take
the Mears Shuttle Service, with
direct service from the Orlando
International Airport. It is cheaper
than renting a car.

FESTIVALS AND EVENTS

1 Central Florida Fair

Early Mar ⓦ centralfloridafair.com

This massive 19-day shindig takes place close to Downtown Orlando (*4603 W. Colonial Dr*), but its cowboy attitude is a world away. The country-style attractions include carnival rides, country music, farming exhibits, and more fried food than you'll ever care to eat.

2 Winter Park Sidewalk Arts Festival

Mid-Mar ⓦ wpsaf.org

For three days, this prestigious outdoor festival in the Winter Park sees hundreds of artists exhibit on sidewalk stalls. Traffic comes to a standstill as the crowds mill around.

3 EPCOT® International Flower & Garden Festival

Mar–May ⓦ disneyworld.com

An annual event at EPCOT® featuring characters ingeniously created from topiary and flowers through-out the park. Everywhere you look, there are gardens filled with blooms of every shape, size, and color. The festival also features demon-strations, tours, and a series of outdoor concerts.

4 Florida Film Festival

Apr ⓦ floridafilmfestival.com

Held at multiple venues across the city, including the Enzian Theater, this ten-day film festival is packed with more than 180 features, documentaries, and shorts. Filmmakers introduce their works, and a few Hollywood names make guest appearances.

5 Orlando International Fringe Festival

May ⓦ orlandofringe.org

With more than 500 performances taking place over 14 days, the Fringe includes improvised comedy, drag shows, stand-up, and more. Inspired by the Edinburgh Fringe, this premier festival event draws enthusiastic local crowds. Loch Haven Park is one of the many venues that hosts this lively festival.

Breakdancers taking to the stage at IMMERSE festival

6 Gay Days

May–Jun ⓦ gaydays.com

Gay Days is a week-long blowout of LGBTQ+ parties and theme park visits, across various venues, for more than 130,000 guests. By day, all visitors here wear a red T-shirt and mix in the parks; at night, parks and clubs are rented out as venues for evening raves. Many hotels also host Gay Days pool parties.

7 EPCOT® International Food & Wine Festival

Aug–Nov ⓦ disneyworld.com

Along with demonstrations, tastings, and events, guests can purchase sample plates of foods from around the world at this international festival held at EPCOT®.

8 IMMERSE – Creative City Project

Oct ⓦ creativecityproject.com

More than 1,000 artists – musicians, dancers, visual artists, theatrical troupes, writers – take part in this annual two-day-and-night collaborative event in Downtown Orlando.

9 International Dragon Boat Festival

Mid-Oct

Steeped in Chinese folklore, this boat festival at Turkey Lake sees more than 70 teams compete. There are 20 paddlers per vessel, with a drummer keeping the strokes in time. Visit the nearby Asia Trend Cultural Expo to learn more about other Asian cultures.

10 Festival of the Trees

Nov

Celebrate the spirit of the holiday season for nine days in November, when the Orlando Museum of Art (p123) is transformed into a winter wonderland. Visitors will glimpse beautifully decorated trees, holiday wreaths, vignettes, and candy-laden gingerbread houses all around the museum.

TOP 10 THEME PARK EVENTS

1. Walt Disney World® Marathon, EPCOT®
Jan
Runners partake in this 26.2-mile (42-km) race around the resort.

2. Mardi Gras, Universal Studios Florida™
Feb–Apr
The ultimate "Big Easy" party, with parades, music, and lots of beads.

3. Grad Bash, Universal Orlando Resort™
Apr
Live concerts, multiple dance parties, and thrill rides for high school seniors.

4. EPCOT's International Food & Wine Festival, EPCOT®
Aug–Nov
Take a tasting tour around the world.

5. Rock the Universe, Universal Orlando Resort™
Sep
Universal's two-night showcase of Christian rock music.

6. Halloween Horror Nights, Universal Studios Florida™
Sep–Nov
Universal is transformed into a ghoulish home for the undead.

7. Mickey's Not-So-Scary Halloween Party, Magic Kingdom®
Sep & Oct
Trick-or-treat through the park for some ghostly family-appropriate fun.

8. Candlelight Processional, EPCOT® World Showcase
Nov & Dec
A celebrity narrator, along with a 50-piece orchestra and choir, tells the story of Christmas.

9. Mickey's Very Merry Christmas Party, Magic Kingdom®
Nov & Dec
A festive parade complete with snow.

10. Grinchmas, Universal's Islands of Adventure™
Dec
Enjoy a live performance of How the Grinch Stole Christmas at Seuss Landing.

DAY TRIPS SOUTH AND WEST

1 Caladesi Island State Park
📍 V5 🏠 1 Causeway Blvd, Dunedin
🕐 8am to sunset daily 🌐 florida stateparks.org

A 3-mile (5-km) island, accessible by ferry from Honeymoon Island, this is a lovely retreat traversed by a nature trail. A ban on cars helps keep it pristine. In season, beach areas are dotted with the tracks of loggerhead turtles that nest here.

2 The Gulf Beaches
Florida's Gulf Coast is strewn with white-sand, low-surf, and warm-water beaches stretching from Pinellas County (Clearwater Beach and St. Pete Beach among others) to Lee County (including Fort Myers Beach, Sanibel and Captiva Islands), on down to Collier County (Naples Beach and Marco Island).

3 Ybor City/Centro Ybor
📍 V5 🏠 Seventh Ave, Tampa
🌐 ybor.org

The Latin heart of Tampa contains the Ybor City Museum State Park plus trendy art galleries and cafés. Try a Cuban sandwich, and strong *café cubano* at the Columbia Restaurant, or dance the night away to salsa and merengue at a lively club.

4 Florida Southern College
Located in Lakeland, 50 miles (80 km) southwest of Orlando, this private college's (p78) architecture is impressive. In 1938, Frank Lloyd Wright was tasked with transforming a lakeside orange grove into a modern campus. The resulting 12 buildings became known as Child of the Sun.

5 Bok Tower Gardens
📍 W6 🏠 1151 Tower Blvd, Lake Wales 🕐 8am–6pm daily
🌐 bohtowergardens.org

This National Historic Landmark has nearly 250 acres (1 sq km) of

North facade of the Bok Tower Gardens

Elephants in ZooTampa at Lowry Park

grounds surrounding a 205-ft (62-m) bell tower and Mediterranean Revival mansion. The visitor center shows a video, and has a museum, café, and gift shop.

6 Busch Gardens®
V5 3000 E. Busch Blvd, Tampa Hours vary, chech website buschgardens.com

With world-class roller coasters, water rides, and numerous other attractions, this park is a close second to Universal's Islands of Adventure™ *(p38)*. Roller coaster enthusiasts rate the park's SheiKra ride very highly – it's a floorless 70-mph (120-km/h) coaster. Nature lovers will enjoy the animal interactions of the Jungala attraction and the truck ride through the plains of the Serengeti Safari. Ask about the free shuttle from Orlando for ticket holders.

7 Salvador Dali Museum
V6 1 Dali Blvd, St. Petersburg 10am–5:30pm Fri–Wed, 10am–8pm Thu thedali.org

One of the world's most comprehensive collections of Salvador Dali's work from 1914 to 1970 can be found at this world-class museum. The art on display includes oils, watercolors, and sculptures by the great Surrealist. There's also a café and an interesting outdoor space.

8 ZooTampa at Lowry Park
V5 1101 W. Sligh Ave, Tampa 9:30am–5pm daily zootampa.org

Tampa's first zoo holds more than 1,300 creatures, including Malayan tigers, African elephants, and Komodo dragons. It also serves as a rehabilitation center for injured manatees and as a sanctuary for Florida panthers and red wolves. Activities such as roller coaster rides, old-fashioned carousels, and a safari ride make for a fun-filled day.

9 Henry B. Plant Museum
V5 410 W. Kennedy Blvd, Tampa 10am–5pm Tue–Sat, noon–5pm Sun plantmuseum.com

In the late 1800s, railroad magnate Henry B. Plant built an opulent Moorish palace in the swamps of Tampa. Now part of the University of Tampa, this museum honors his life. Take a tour through its restored rooms.

10 Florida Aquarium
V5 701 Channelside Dr, Tampa 9:30am–5pm daily flaquarium.org

Florida's native species are just a fraction of more than 10,000 animals and plants here. Wetlands, bays, coral reefs, and their inhabitants are featured in several galleries. You can watch divers feed marine creatures.

DAY TRIPS NORTH AND EAST

1 Cocoa Beach
📍 X5

Just 60 miles (96 km) east of I-4 via the Beachline Expressway, picturesque Cocoa Beach is the seashore closest to Orlando. The lengthy stretch of golden sand and the surf are the main reasons visitors flock to this laid-back seaside town.

2 Daytona Beach
📍 X4 🌐 daytonabeach.com

During the annual Spring Break, this legendary beach (just 90 minutes from Orlando along I-4) is the destination for thousands of vacationing college students. Beach Street is also lined with shops, restaurants, and clubs; and of course, there's also the Daytona Speedway, home to the Daytona 500 and other NASCAR races.

3 New Smyrna Beach
📍 X4

Just south of Daytona Beach, New Smyrna is a smaller, calmer town. The white-sand beach is picture perfect – but as at Daytona, cars share the space with sunworshipers. For food, the place to go is JB's Fish Camp, a raucous and friendly shack beside Mosquito Lagoon, serving some of the state's tastiest fish, seafood, and key lime pie.

4 Sebastian Inlet
📍 X6

Located 15 miles (24 km) south of Melbourne, Sebastian Inlet's waves

Atlantic Ocean

- ✈ 6 Fernandina Beach
- Jacksonville
- Ponte Vedra Beach
- (A1A)
- 9 St. Augustine
- Palatka
- Marineland
- Flagler Beach
- (A1A)
- Ormond Beach
- 2 Daytona Beach
- DeLand
- 3 New Smyrna Beach
- 10
- Mount Dora
- 5 Sanford
- Titusville
- 7
- Clermont
- Orlando
- 8
- Celebration
- Cocoa
- 1 Cocoa Beach
- Kissimmee
- Melbourne
- (A1A)
- Lakeland
- 4 Sebastian
- 0 km   50
- 0 miles   50

The spectacular Cocoa Beach pier

draw surfers from near and far, with several major competitions held here each year. It's also a good saltwater fishing spot. History buffs can explore the McLarty Treasure Museum and the Sebastian Fishing Museum.

5 Mount Dora
🅟 W4 🆆 ci.mount-dora.fl.us
Charming Mount Dora's local industry focuses on antiques, such as Reninger's Antique & Flea Markets and the small shops on and around Donnelly Street. There is a guided tour ride on the trolley and boating opportunities.

6 Amelia Island
Set off the northeastern coast, this pristine barrier island offers 13 miles (21 km) of sugary white-sand beaches, a charming historic district filled with boutiques and bistros, and activities to keep you busy, including fishing, boating, golfing, hiking, and biking along the island trails.

7 Merritt Island National Wildlife Refuge
This 140,000-acre (567-sq-km) wildlife sanctuary (p48), which is the second largest in Florida, has more federally endangered species than any other refuge in the United States. A 7-mile (11-km) driving tour with shaded boardwalks weaves through lush pine and oak hammocks.

Alligator at the Merritt Island National Wildlife Refuge

Atlantis Orbiter, Kennedy Space Center Visitor Complex

8 Kennedy Space Center Visitor Complex
This well-conceived monument (p52) to America's space program showcases mammoth exhibits, such as the Saturn V Rocket, and smaller items like old space suits. Bus tours are a good way to take in the installations.

9 St. Augustine
Influenced by the Spanish Conquistadors, the Timucua, and even the British, St. Augustine has over 60 historic sites, including the Castillo de San Marco and Fort Matanzas. There are many independently owned restaurants and quaint boutiques with live music often filling the air. Explore by a hop-on hop-off trolley tour. The lighthouse is said to be one of the most haunted sites in the U.S.

10 Blue Spring State Park
🅟 W4 🅐 2100 French Ave, Orange City 🕒 8am–sunset daily 🆆 florida stateparks.org/park/Blue-Spring 🅷
Located 33 miles (53 km) north of Orlando, Blue Spring State Park is the largest spring on the St. Johns River. Covering more than 2,600 acres (10.5 sq km), this manatee refuge offers pale blue waters and lush forested banks. There's also a boardwalk built specifically for viewing the underwater wildlife from a safe distance.

AREA BY AREA

Walt Disney World® Resort
and Lake Buena Vista   98

International Drive Area   108

Kissimmee and Beyond   116

Downtown Orlando   122

Winter Park, Maitland, and
Eatonville   130

Hollywood Boulevard set, Universal Studios Florida™

WALT DISNEY WORLD® RESORT AND LAKE BUENA VISTA

There was just one drawback to California's Disneyland®, Walt Disney's first theme park, which opened in 1955: there was no space around the park in which to expand. Following an aerial tour of Central Florida in 1965, Disney began to buy large tracts of land, which consisted of citrus groves and swamps. Today, the 47-sq-mile (121-sq-km) Walt Disney World® Resort contains four major theme parks, two water parks, several smaller attractions, and hotels and resorts, which spill over into the adjoining Lake Buena Vista area.

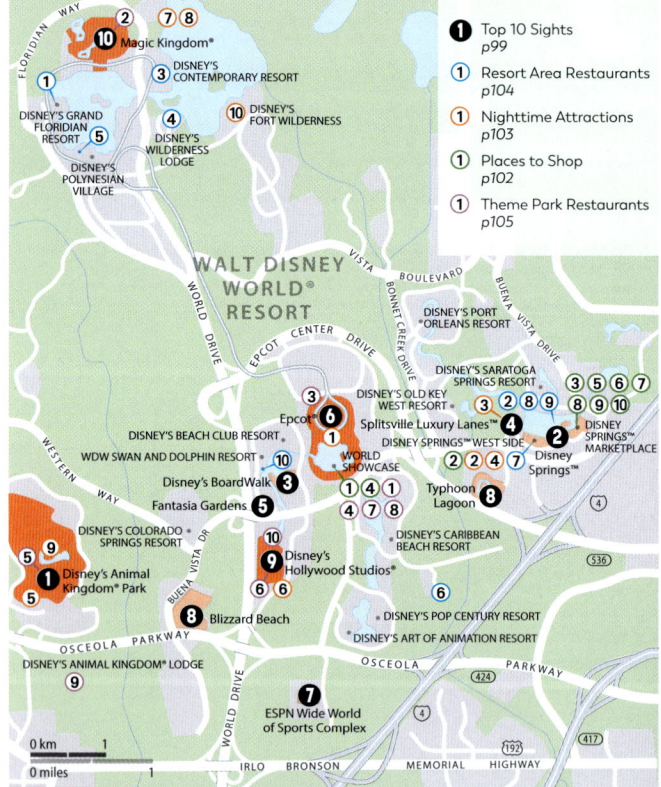

1 Top 10 Sights
p99

1 Resort Area Restaurants
p104

1 Nighttime Attractions
p103

1 Places to Shop
p102

1 Theme Park Restaurants
p105

For places to stay in this area, see p148

Herd of giraffes at Disney's Animal Kingdom® Park

1 Disney's Animal Kingdom® Park

Disney's fourth Orlando park *(p32)* is a place where animals from around the world roam within a host of landscapes.

2 Disney Springs™

📍 X2 🌐 disneysprings.com

With specially created waterways, bubbling springs (hence the name), and themed neighborhoods, this shopping, dining, and entertainment district is an attraction in itself. Each neighborhood has its own array of stores and eating places, with the Town Center hosting particularly high-end retailers and signature restaurants. The Marketplace is the most family-friendly area, with a variety of kids' shops, the occasional free concert, and casual counter-service restaurants. The Landing offers more upscale dining, with THE BOATHOUSE® *(p104)* among the notable restaurants. West Side has a cluster of entertainment venues, along with some eclectic shops.

3 Disney's BoardWalk

📍 W2 🏠 2101 EPCOT® Resorts Blvd 🌐 disneyworld.disney.go.com

Disney's BoardWalk is designed to reflect the splendor of the original boardwalks set along the Atlantic seaboard in the 19th century. Next to the Victorian-style Disney's BoardWalk Inn & Villas, and only a short distance from the Swan & Dolphin and Disney's Beach & Yacht Club resorts, this popular dining and entertainment district is constantly bustling with activity. Wrapping around Crescent Lake, it features a number of Disney's most popular restaurants, such as the famed Morimoto Asia *(p104)*. Completing the nostalgic scene is an ice-cream shop, pizza window, and at night expect to see street performers and boardwalk games added to the mix. Just across the lake is EPCOT®, and the nearby lawn is a perfect spot for sitting to watch its nighttime fireworks display. Surrey bikes are also popular here, with seating for two, four, or six – you can bike around the lake and back.

4 Splitsville Luxury Lanes™

📍 X2 🏠 Disney Springs™ West Side 🕐 Hours vary, chech website 🌐 splitsvillelanes.com

This bowling alley in Disney Springs™ is spread across two levels spanning an area of 50,000 sq ft (4,645 sq m). Teams have access to 30 luxury lanes and a varied menu of food, served lane-side. Other than this, there is an outdoor patio area where you can relax, as well as large-screen TVs and pool tables.

5 Fantasia Gardens
📍 W2–W3 🕐 10am–11pm daily
🌐 disneyworld.disney.go.com 🔗

Orlando in general and Walt Disney World® Resort in particular have some great golf courses *(p72)*. Two miniature golf courses – Fantasia Gardens and Winter Summerland – offer a total of 72 holes of putting fun. Inspired by the classic Disney cartoon *Fantasia*, Fantasia Gardens' 18 holes have an animal theme. Located near Disney's Hollywood Studios®, it's the more forgiving of the two courses, and so the better choice for young kids or beginners. Winter Summerland is a scale model of a full-size course, complete with bunkers, water hazards, frustrating putting greens, and holes that are up to 75 ft (23 m) long. Here you can choose between the winter- and summer-themed courses.

6 EPCOT®
The developers at Walt Disney knew a park had to appeal to curious adults and techno kids. EPCOT® *(p26)*, as a result, is a celebration of technology and culture – its fascinating World Swhocase Pavilions are a highlight of the park.

WALT DISNEY

Despite great success in the film world, Walter Elias Disney had his sights set on more than just animation. He was the man who created the theme park, a place where visitors can spin their own story in a safe and upbeat environment. His first, California's Disneyland® Park, was the only park that came to fruition before his death in 1966, 11 years after it opened.

7 ESPN Wide World of Sports Complex
📍 W3 🕐 Hours vary, check website
🌐 espnwwos.com 🔗

Disney's sports complex is the spring training home of Major League baseball's Atlanta Braves (Feb–Mar) and minor league baseball's Orlando Rays, a farm team for the Tampa Bay Devil

Striking Spaceship Earth at the entrance to EPCOT®

Rays (Apr–Sep). The complex is also a winter home for basketball's Harlem Globetrotters. Other facilities in the complex include a fitness center; basketball, volleyball, and tennis courts; softball, soccer, and lacrosse fields; a martial-arts venue; and a golf driving range. There is an extreme sports area catering for skateboarders, in-line skaters, and cyclists, which is also open for special events.

8 Water Parks
🅟 W3 & X2 🅦 disneyworld. disney.go.com ↗

Walt Disney World® has two water parks. Typhoon Lagoon is designed to resemble a beach resort devastated by a tropical storm, can hold more than 7,000 people at once, and has plenty of rides and attractions. Blizzard Beach imagines a melted ski resort. Both parks have similar features: long drops to build up speed and darkened tubes to confuse you before spilling you into a wading pool below. The parks have seasonal hours, so call to check.

Twilight Zone Tower of Terror™, Disney's Hollywood Studios®

9 Disney's Hollywood Studios®
A park *(p30)* that combines front-of-house fun with behind-the-scenes explanation. It is also home to some of Disney's most intense thrill rides.

10 Magic Kingdom®
Who's the leader of the theme-park pack? Disney's first Florida park *(p22)* is the most popular in the U.S.

HIDDEN MICKEYS

Hidden Mickeys started many years ago as a joke among park designers. Today these silhouettes of Mickey's ears, his head, or his whole body, semi-hidden throughout the parks and resorts, are a Disney tradition. They can be anywhere: in the landscaping, in the murals, and even overhead, for example on the Earffel Tower in Disney's Hollywood Studios®. See how many you can spot *(hiddenmickeys.org)*.

The colorful LEGO® Store, Disney Springs™

Places to Shop

1. House of Good Fortune
🔲 W2 🏠 China Pavilion, World Showcase, EPCOT®
Here's an excellent source for all things Asian, from jade figurines to silk robes, and furnishings to wind chimes.

2. Pop Gallery
🔲 X2 🏠 The Landing at Disney Springs™
Original works of art are showcased and sold at the gallery, including paintings, glassware, and gift items.

3. The LEGO® Store
🔲 X2 🏠 Disney Springs™ Marketplace
Kids love the play area at this store, which has enough LEGO® pieces to build almost anything.

4. Mitsukoshi Department Store
🔲 W2 🏠 Japan Pavilion, World Showcase, EPCOT®
Kimonos, swords, bonsais, Japanese Disneyana, and kites are sold here.

5. Twenty Eight & Main
🔲 X2 🏠 Disney Springs™ Marketplace
A boutique offering vintage-inspired gentlemen's clothing and accessories.

6. Basin
🔲 X2 🏠 Disney Springs™ Marketplace
Shop for bath bombs, scented soaps, and natural skin-care products at Basin.

7. Art of Disney
🔲 X2 🏠 Disney Springs™ Marketplace
This one-of-a-kind gallery is filled with Disney sculptures, animation cels (celluloid sheets used for films), and other collectibles.

8. Once Upon a Toy
🔲 X2 🏠 Disney Springs™ Marketplace
Step back in time for old-style toys like Lincoln Logs and Mr. Potato Head, progressing via a build-your-own *Star Wars* light saber to modern games.

9. Tren-D
🔲 X2 🏠 Disney Springs™ Marketplace
Tren-D has stylish apparel, accessories, and creations by cutting-edge designers.

10. World of Disney®
🔲 X2 🏠 Disney Springs™ Marketplace
The Disney store to beat all stores – over 51,000 sq ft (4,738 sq m) brimming with clothing, jewelry, toys, and souvenirs, plus the Bibiddi Bobiddi salon for all aspiring princes and princesses.

Nighttime Attractions

1. Luminous: The Symphony of Us
W2 World Showcase Lagoon, EPCOT® disneyworld.disney.go.com
A nightly explosion of lasers, fireworks, and fountains over the lagoon is set to music at this show, celebrating the world's diverse cultures.

2. AMC® Disney Springs™ 24
X2 Disney Springs™ West Side amctheatres.com
Twenty-four screens show the latest box office hits. There's also a massive ETX auditorium and several Fork & Screen® dine-in theaters.

3. Splitsville Luxury Lanes
A 1950s-themed bowling alley complex *(p99)*, with several bars and restaurants, as well as 30 high-tech lanes.

4. House of Blues®
X2 Disney Springs™ West Side houseofblues.com
One of Orlando's best venues for live music, hosting a wide variety of acts in various genres.

5. Pandora – The World of Avatar
Disney's imagineers bring to life the sights of Pandora (from James Cameron's movie, *Avatar*) here *(p32)*. This mythical land becomes a glowing wonderland at night.

6. Fantasmic!
W3 Disney's Hollywood Studios® disneyworld.disney.go.com
Featuring a cast of favorite characters, this wonderful evening show is set in a huge outdoor theater with a stage surrounded by water.

7. Disney Enchantment
V1 Magic Kingdom®
The skies above Cinderella Castle are sprinkled with fireworks set to music, while a magical projection takes over the castle itself.

8. Electrical Water Pageant
W1 Seven Seas Lagoon, Bay Lake, Magic Kingdom®
A parade of illuminated creatures atop floating barges that ply the waters in front of the Magic Kingdom® resorts.

9. Tree of Life Awakenings
V3 Disney's Animal Kingdom® disneyworld.disney.go.com
On select nights, light projections are cast against one of the park's most iconic symbols, the Tree of Life. In a celebratory fashion, animated animal spirits inspired by *The Lion King* spring to life accompanied by music.

10. Hoop-Dee-Doo Musical Revue
W1 Disney's Fort Wilderness Resort 6:15 & 8pm nightly disneyworld.disney.go.com
This show combines an all-you-can-eat dinner with Country & Western dancing, singing, and comedy.

The Tree of Life, in Disney's Animal Kingdom®

Resort Area Restaurants

1. Victoria & Albert's
📍 V1 🏠 Disney's Grand Floridian Resort & Spa 🌐 disneyworld.disney.go.com · $$$

One of Disney's most exclusive dining options, this romantic gem has an international menu served by attentive waitstaff. It's located on the second floor of Disney's Grand Floridian Resort & Spa.

2. T-REX™
📍 X2 🏠 Disney Springs™ 🌐 trexcafe.com · $$

This dinosaur-themed café serves delicious all-American fare in a fun, interactive setting. There are also a variety of hands-on discovery zones.

3. California Grill
📍 W1 🏠 Disney's Contemporary Resort 🌐 disneyworld.disney.go.com · $$$

This vegetarian-friendly restaurant on the 15th floor serves California cuisine in a romantic space. Book a table by the panoramic windows for dinner with a view of Magic Kingdom® Park's Cinderella Castle.

4. Whispering Canyon
📍 W1 🏠 Disney's Wilderness Lodge 🌐 disneyworld.disney.go.com · $$

Sample hearty Western fare at this charming family restaurant. The all-you-care-to-enjoy menu has a good range of kid-friendly options; plant-based dishes are also available.

5. 'Ohana
📍 V1 🏠 Disney's Polynesian Village Resort 🌐 disneyworld.disney.go.com · $$$

Enjoy games, storytelling, and hula dancing at this popular Hawaiian-style diner, which specializes in skewer service. The breakfast menu featuring delicious waffles and fresh fruit is equally tempting.

6. Bull & Bear Steakhouse
📍 X3 🏠 14200 Bonnet Creek Ln 🌐 bullandbearorlando.com · $$$

Modeled after the original in New York, this elegant restaurant in the Waldorf Astoria has a high-end menu and impeccable service.

7. Summer House on the Lake
📍 X2 🏠 Disney Springs™ 🌐 disneysprings.com · $$

This airy waterside restaurant serves Californian-style dishes made with a host of seasonal ingredients. Enjoy your meal either inside or on one of the scenic patios overlooking the breezy lake.

8. THE BOATHOUSE®
📍 X2 🏠 Disney Springs™ 🌐 theboathouseorlando.com · $$$

Meat and seafood entrees and appetizers are on the award-winning menu at this nautical themed restaurant. You can also take a trip on one of the Dream Boats™ from the 1930s, 1940s, and 1950s. Reservations are highly recommended.

9. Morimoto Asia
📍 X2 🏠 Disney Springs™ 🌐 morimotoasia.com · $$

Experience the finest in modern Pan-Asian cuisine as envisioned by famed Japanese chef Morimoto at this striking restaurant. Sushi, ribs, and other specialties from China, Japan, and Korea line the menu.

10. Todd English's bluezoo
📍 W2 🏠 Dolphin Hotel, 1500 EPCOT® Resorts Blvd, Lake Buena Vista 🌐 swandolphin.com · $$$

Guests at this underwater-themed restaurant can savor locally sourced seafood, plus tasty chicken, beef, and pork dishes. The two-pound Maine "Cantonese" lobster is a highlight on the menu.

Theme Park Restaurants

PRICE CATEGORIES

For a three-course meal for one, a glass of house wine, and all unavoidable extra charges including tax.

$ under $30 $$ $30–60 $$$ over $60

The dining area of Tiffins, Disney's Animal Kingdom®

1. Via Napoli Ristorante e Pizzeria
W2 Italy Pavilion, EPCOT®
disneyworld.disney.go.com · $$
Pizzas are made with Italian ingredients and cooked in giant wood-fire ovens at this lively pizzeria.

2. Cinderella's Royal Table
V1 Magic Kingdom® disney world.disney.go.com · $$$
Meet the princesses and Fairy Godmother while dining inside Cinderella's castle. Book ahead.

3. Coral Reef Restaurant
W2 Living Seas Pavilion, EPCOT®
disneyworld.disney.go.com · $$$
Enjoy seafood, meat, and vegetarian dishes on the seasonal menu here against a fabulous backdrop of a living coral reef.

4. Le Cellier Steakhouse
W2 Canadian Pavilion, EPCOT®
disneyworld.disney.go.com · $$$
Dine on prime meats, seafood, and poutine at this steakhouse inspired by the wine cellars of a grand château.

5. Tiffins
V3 Disney's Animal Kingdom®
disneyworld.disney.go.com · $$$
The three dining rooms here serve tasty Asian, African, and Latin dishes.

6. Sci-Fi Dine-In Theater Restaurant
W3 Disney's Hollywood Studios®
universalorlando.com · $$
Watch movie clips from a car-shaped booth while enjoying all-American cuisine at this restaurant.

7. San Angel Inn
W2 Mexico Pavilion, EPCOT®
disneyworld.disney.go.com · $$$
Try traditional dishes like *mole poblano* (chicken with spices and chocolate) or beef with black beans and fried plantain at this massive Mexican restaurant.

8. Rainforest Cafe
W2 505 Rain Forest Rd, Lake Buena Vista rainforestcafe.com · $$
At this jungle-inspired spot, every meal is accompanied by animated animals and lively sound effects.

9. Boma – Flavors of Africa
V3 Disney's Animal Kingdom Lodge disneyworld.disney.go.com · $$$
Enjoy an African dinner buffet at this restaurant – one of Disney's most popular – where the tables are made from huge tree trunks. There's also a children's buffet.

10. 50's Prime Time Café
W3 Disney's Hollywood Studios®
disneyworld.disney.go.com · $$
Watch 1950s kitsch and vintage TV reruns here as you dine on classic American comfort food – meatloaf, pot roast, and fried chicken.

Disney Enchantment fireworks at Magic Kingdom® Park

INTERNATIONAL DRIVE AREA

International Drive is a brash and busy 10-mile (16-km) parkway featuring three major theme parks, countless smaller attractions, and the U.S.A.'s second-largest convention center, with Universal's theme parks and entertainment complex right nearby. Added to the mix are hundreds of hotels and resorts catering to all budgets, shopping malls and outlet stores, and themed, casual, and fast-food restaurants.

1 2 3 4 5 6 7
The Wizarding World of Harry Potter™ (Diagon Alley™) 3
Universal Studios Florida™ 1
The Wizarding World of Harry Potter™ (Hogsmeade™) 3
6 8 9 10 4
Universal's Islands of Adventure™
CITYWALK™ 3 3 5 10
Fun Spot America 8
Titanic: The Artifact Exhibition 5
Ripley's Believe It or Not!® Odditorium
WonderWorks
POINTE ORLANDO
Aquatica 7
SeaWorld® Orlando 9
Discovery Cove® 2

1 **Top 10 Sights** p109

1 Places to Eat p115

1 Bars, Clubs, and Entertainment p114

1 Diagon Alley™ and Hogsmeade™ Shops and Stores p113

1 Eye-Openers on I-Drive p112

For places to stay in this area, see p149

1 Universal Studios Florida™

Part studio and part attraction, the movie-themed rides and shows here (p34) really let visitors step inside the motion pictures.

2 Discovery Cove®

📍 T6 🏠 6000 Discovery Cove Way® 🕐 9am–5pm daily 🌐 discoverycove.com ↗

You might be in land-locked Orlando, but you can still fulfill those tropical island fantasies of snorkeling over coral reefs if you check in to Discovery Cove®. Visitors flock here for the white-sand beaches, snorkeling opportunities in fresh and saltwater lagoons, and relaxed beach-resort vibe. Admission is not cheap (largely because there are never more than 1,000 visitors daily), but you get almost everything you need for the day thrown in, including sun block, lunch, and snorkel gear, as well as a 7-day pass to SeaWorld® (p111). Kids might miss the thrill rides, but they will not be short of things to do.

3 The Wizarding World of Harry Potter™

The addition of Hogsmeade™ to Universal's Islands of Adventure™ and Diagon Alley™ to Universal Studios Florida™ – the two linked by the magical Hogwarts™ Express – has cast its own spell over visitors, making Universal's parks (p42) more popular than ever.

Thrilling river rafting ride, Universal's Islands of Adventure™

4 Universal's Islands of Adventure™

Spider-Man, The Hulk, Dr. Seuss, and the dinosaurs of Jurassic Park rule here (p38), with wild rides dedicated to each.

5 Titanic: The Artifact Exhibition

📍 T3 🏠 7324 International Dr 🕐 11am–10pm daily 🌐 titanic orlando.com ↗

This exhibit's 200 artifacts include a life jacket and an old deck chair, both recovered from the wreckage of the fateful liner, as well as the *Titanic*'s second-class passenger list. The attraction also has full-scale re-creations of some of the ship's interior, including its grand staircase, as well as a collection of memorabilia from three major *Titanic* movies – including one of the costumes worn by Leonardo DiCaprio. Actors in period garb play out events that occurred on the ill-fated voyage, telling the story of the White Star Line's supposedly unsinkable ship. Most of the artifacts came out of private collections in both the United Kingdom and the U.S.A.

Hogwarts™ castle, The Wizarding World of Harry Potter™

Walkabout Waters, the rain fortress at Aquatica®

6 WonderWorks

📍 T4 🏠 Pointe Orlando, 9067 International Dr 🕐 9am–midnight daily 🔵 wonderworksonline.com ↗

You can't miss this attraction from the outside: it looks as though a classical building has landed upside down on top of a warehouse. Inside, there are 85 hands-on exhibits. Highlights include an earthquake simulator; a Bridge of Fire, where you can literally experience the hair-raising effects of 250,000 watts of static electricity; and Virtual Hoops, which uses cinema technology to put you on TV to play basketball against one of the NBA's top players. You can also try virtual hang gliding, which sends you soaring like a bird through the Grand Canyon, and the WonderCoaster, which challenges your roller coaster-designing skills and then your nerve to ride your creation

Astronaut space suit, WonderWorks

in a simulator. WonderWorks also runs a laser-tag venue and a twice-nightly magic show, both of which cost extra.

7 Aquatica®

📍 U5 🏠 5800 Water Play Way, International Dr 🕐 10am–5pm daily, with extended seasonal hours 🔵 aquatica.com/orlando ↗

SeaWorld®'s eco-themed water park, just across from SeaWorld® itself, makes a big splash with families and thrill-seekers alike. It combines wild slides and rides, including an eight-person racing slide, with a number of tot-friendly options. The park has a whimsical South Pacific setting,

I-RIDE TROLLEY

One of the best things about I-Drive itself is the tourist-oriented I-Ride Trolley (p139), which offers an easy and affordable way to see some of the area's oddities, while avoiding the I-Drive's heavy traffic or walking any distance in the intense heat. There are 78 stops on the circuit, serving all the local major attractions, shopping malls, hotels, and restaurants.

SEAWORLD® CONTROVERSY

SeaWorld® has a rehabilitation program of rescuing stranded marine animals. However, less positive aspects of SeaWorld® have come to light since the release of the 2013 documentary film *Blackfish*, which questioned the ethics of keeping killer whales in captivity. In 2016, SeaWorld® announced it would end its orca whale breeding and performance program, but the park continues to receive strong criticism, seeing a downturn in public opinion and a drop in visitor numbers.

which makes the perfect backdrop for up-close encounters with the park's wilder inhabitants, including brightly colored tropical fish, macaws, and African spurred tortoises. A stretch of white sand sits adjacent to giant wave pools, while a winding river takes riders bobbing along the waterways of Loggerhead Lane. You can also rent cabanas in various sizes in advance.

8 Fun Spot America
📍 U2 🏠 5500 Fun Spot Way 🕐 2pm–midnight, with extended seasonal and weekend hours 🌐 fun-spot.com

This arcade/amusement park has something for everyone, with four go-kart tracks, two giant roller coasters, and the world's biggest SkyCoaster. There are bumper boats and cars, a Ferris wheel, arcade games, and a kid zone that has swings, a train, spinning tea cups, and flying bears.

9 SeaWorld® Orlando
📍 T5 🏠 7007 SeaWorld® Dr 🕐 9am–6pm daily 🌐 seaworld. com ↗

While home to some of the wildest rides in all of Orlando (Mako®, Manta, and Kraken®), the majority of the park is dedicated to life under the sea. With exhibits dedicated to sharks, penguins,

whales, manatees, and more, this park is unlike any other around. Its grounds are meticulously landscaped, with towering palm trees, a central lake, and blooming flowers at every turn.

10 Ripley's Believe It or Not!® Odditorium
📍 T3 🏠 8201 International Dr 🕐 9am–midnight daily 🌐 ripleys. com ↗

If you're a fan of the bizarre, you'll love Ripley's. This worldwide chain of attractions displays the unbelievable finds of Robert Ripley's 40 years of adventures, the reports of which were published in more than 300 newspapers and read by more than 80 million people. The Orlando branch has 16 themed galleries with over 600 exhibits and artifacts, such as a full-scale model of a 1907 Silver Ghost Rolls Royce (with moving engine parts) built out of 1,016,711 matchsticks and 63 pints (36 litres) of glue; a wild spinning vortex tunnel; a flute made of human bones; a mosaic of the *Mona Lisa* made of toast; shrunken heads; a five-legged cow; and a portrait of Van Gogh made from 3,000 postcards.

Entrance to Ripley's Believe It or Not!® Odditorium

Beautifully illuminated Ferris wheel, ICON Orlando 360™

Eye-Openers on I-Drive

1. Four Points by Sheraton Orlando Studio City
📍 T2 🏠 5905 International Dr
🌐 marriott.com

This distinctive 21-story circular hotel has a huge globe sitting on top.

2. Madame Tussauds
📍 T3 🏠 8401 International Dr
🕐 11am–5pm Sun–Thu, 11am–6pm Fri & Sat 🌐 madametussauds.com

Celebrity waxworks here range from Queen Elizabeth II to Marilyn Monroe.

3. Hollywood Drive-In Golf
📍 T1 🏠 6000 Universal Blvd, Universal® Orlando 🕐 9am–midnight daily 🌐 hollywooddriveingolf.com

Fun 1950s-B-movie-inspired inter-active mini-golf courses offering graveyard and flying saucer themes.

4. Kings Dining & Entertainment
📍 T3 🏠 8255 S. International Dr
🕐 2pm–midnight Mon–Thu, noon–1am Fri & Sat, 11:30am–10pm Sun
🌐 playathings.com

Modern venue with 22 bowling lanes, along with two bars, a restaurant, and 60 giant TVs.

5. ICON Orlando 360™
📍 T3 🏠 8401 International Dr
🕐 Hours vary, chech website
🌐 iconparkorlando.com

Giant Ferris wheel offering a bird's-eye view of the city as it slowly revolves.

6. ICEBAR
Enjoy karaoke and swing dance lessons at this frozen cocktail bar (p114).

7. Ripley's Believe It or Not®! Odditorium
Fantastic objects and movie footage of strange feats can be seen here (p111).

8. iFLY Orlando
📍 T2 🏠 6805 Visitors Cir 🕐 Hours vary, chech website 🌐 iflyworld.com

Experience the thrill of virtual skydiving.

9. WonderWorks
Amusement park (p110) with exhibits that are fun and educational for all ages.

10. Dezerland Park
📍 U2 🏠 5250 International Dr
🕐 9:30am–8pm daily 🌐 dezerlandpark.com

Recreation center with go-karts, a cinema, bowling alley, and mini-golf.

Diagon Alley™ and Hogsmeade™ Shops and Stores

1. Weasleys' Wizard Wheezes™
🔵 T1 🏠 Diagon Alley™
Skiving snackboxes, extendable ears, and love potions are on offer at this unique little joke shop.

2. Borgin and Burkes™
🔵 T1 🏠 Diagon Alley™
Down crooked Nocturn Alley, just off Diagon Alley™, this shop with dusty windows is filled with items infused with dark magic – including the hand of glory and poisonous potions.

3. Magical Menagerie™
🔵 T1 🏠 Diagon Alley™
Lining the shelves here is every sort of stuffed toys you could imagine. Soft plush versions of everyone's favorites are available for purchase, including Crookshanks the cat, Hedwig the owl, and Buckbeak the hippogriff.

4. Quality Quidditch™ Supplies
🔵 T1 🏠 Diagon Alley™
You'll find everything you need for a game of Quidditch at this store, whether that's a bludger, a quaffle, a snitch, or the appropriate robes. They're well stocked on brooms, so be sure to pick up your Nimbus 2001.

5. Wiseacre's Wizarding Equipment
🔵 T1 🏠 Diagon Alley™
This celestial-inspired shop, with an ethereal star-filled sky painted upon the ceiling, is stocked with crystal balls, telescopes, binoculars, compasses, and time turners.

6. Ollivanders™
Every Harry Potter fan knows that the wand chooses the wizard at Ollivanders™. It has branches in both Hogsmeade™ and Diagon Alley™ *(p43)*.

7. Madam Malkin's Robes for All Occasions
🔵 T1 🏠 Diagon Alley™
Here, you can pick up your Hogwarts school uniform ties, scarves, and cardigans, a new wizard hat, and goodies bearing the logos of Hogwarts' houses.

8. Honeydukes™
🔵 T1 🏠 Hogsmeade™
The shelves at Honeydukes™ are stacked with brightly colored sweets and treats, like pepper imps, Bertie Bots Every Flavor Beans, treacle fudge, acid pops, cauldron cakes, and chocolate frogs.

9. Filch's Emporium™ of Confiscated Goods
🔵 T1 🏠 Hogsmeade™
Most confiscated items are not for sale, but you'll find an array of Quidditch clothing and accessories, chess sets, magical creatures, and souvenirs galore.

10. Dervish and Banges™
🔵 T1 🏠 Hogsmeade™
Shop for magical items such as Sneakoscopes, Spectrespecs, Omnioculars, and *The Monster Book of Monsters* here. Hogwarts uniforms and clothing are also available.

Wide range of treats and sweets at Honeydukes™

Bars, Clubs, and Entertainment

Signage at the Bob Marley – A Tribute to Freedom venue

1. Lucky Leprechaun
📍 T3 🏠 7032 International Dr 📞 407-352-7031

There's karaoke every night at this Irish-themed bar with a great selection of Irish beers.

2. The Vault 5421: Gods and Monsters
📍 U2 🏠 5421 International Dr Ⓦ godmonsters.com

You'll find retro games, costume nights, pop-ups, esoteric drinks, and mead here.

3. Jimmy Buffet's Margaritaville
📍 T1 🏠 CityWalk™ Ⓦ margaritaville orlando.com

A hub for Parrot Heads or anyone who wants to enjoy great drinks, good food, and live entertainment.

4. Howl at the Moon
📍 T4 🏠 8815 International Dr Ⓦ howlatthemoon.com

Rock 'n' roll dueling pianos and signature drinks make this high-energy nightclub a fun adult getaway.

5. Bob Marley – A Tribute to Freedom
📍 T1 🏠 CityWalk™ Ⓦ universal orlando.com

Live reggae music is the draw here – the bands are usually excellent. Only over-21s are allowed entry after 10pm.

6. Cuba Libre Rum Bar
📍 T4 🏠 9101 International Dr Ⓦ cubalibrerestaurant.com

DJs spin lively Latin tunes at Cuba Libre, where salsa, merengue, and bachata reign late at night.

7. ICEBAR
📍 T4 🏠 8967 International Dr Ⓦ icebarorlando.com

This bar is made completely of ice – warm down coats are provided at the entrance. Time inside this small venue is limited, but there's a lounge outside to party the night away. Only over-21s can enter the bar after 9pm.

8. Mango's Tropical Cafe
📍 T3 🏠 8126 International Dr Ⓦ mangos.com/mangos-orlando

This club has fabulous live dance performances through the night.

9. The Whiskey
📍 S3 🏠 7563 W. Sand Lake Rd Ⓦ downatthewhiskey.com

Enjoy rare whiskeys and expertly crafted cocktails here, along with award-winning burgers.

10. Red Coconut Club
📍 T1 🏠 CityWalk™ Ⓦ universal orlando.com

Hip 1950s retro lounge with three bars on two levels, plus live music and DJs. Choose one of the signature martinis.

Lovely vintage decor at Cuba Libre Rum Bar

Places to Eat

1. Del Frisco's Double Eagle Steakhouse

⓿ T4 🏠 9150 International Dr Ⓦ delfriscos.com · $$$

Sample delicious seafood and steaks at this famous and chic chain restaurant. The wine list is excellent, too.

2. Texas de Brazil Churrascaria

⓿ U2 🏠 5259 International Dr Ⓦ texasdebrazil.com · $$$

This all-you-can-eat Brazilian steakhouse offers a wide range of meats and a great salad bar.

3. Maggiano's Little Italy

⓿ T4 🏠 9101 International Dr Ⓦ maggianos.com · $$

On the menu at this spot are generous portions of traditional Italian dishes.

4. Everglades

⓿ T3 🏠 9840 International Dr Ⓦ evergladesrestaurant.com · $$$

A casual hotel restaurant, Everglades serves superb steaks and seafood.

5. Seasons 52

⓿ S3 🏠 7700 W. Sand Lake Rd Ⓦ seasons52.com · $$

The low-calorie seasonal menu here features mouthwatering dishes such as crab-stuffed mushrooms.

6. Oceanaire Seafood Room

⓿ T4 🏠 9101 International Dr Ⓦ theoceanaire.com · $$$

The best seafood and prime meats are served at this elegant restaurant. The cocktails are excellent.

7. Capital Grille

⓿ T4 🏠 9101 International Dr Ⓦ thecapitalgrille.com · $$$

Another refined, high-end restaurant, Capital Grille specializes in prime grilled meats.

8. Café Tu Tu Tango

⓿ T3 🏠 8625 International Dr Ⓦ cafetututango.com · $$

Local artists' work adorns the walls of this Barcelona-inspired café. Dishes include black bean soup, shrimp fritters, and quesadillas.

9. Cuba Libre

⓿ T4 🏠 9101 International Dr Ⓦ cubalibrerestaurant.com · $$$

This open-air restaurant has a tropical atmosphere, lively Latin music, and a menu of contemporary Cuban cuisine. If that's not enough, there's also late-night salsa dancing.

10. The Palm

⓿ T1 🏠 Hard Rock Hotel, 5800 Universal Blvd Ⓦ thepalm.com · $$$

The specialty is high-end steaks, often belly-busters up to a 36-oz (1.2-kg) strip for two – but don't overlook the lobster option.

The upscale Capital Grille steakhouse

KISSIMMEE AND BEYOND

What used to be a ranch town has in the past few decades evolved into a hotel enclave for Walt Disney World® tourists. But there's much more to Kissimmee. While U.S.-192 (also called the Irlo Bronson Memorial Highway) is dense with strip malls and hotels, downtown Kissimmee (centered on Broadway and Emmet) was built in the early 1890s and features low-slung buildings. The relatively undeveloped land around the highway offers access to Florida's natural beauty.

1 LEGOLAND®

Built on part of the former site of Cypress Gardens, Florida's oldest theme park (p44) has captured everyone's imagination. This 150-acre (60-ha) interactive theme park is located just 45 minutes from Orlando and is dedicated to families and children between the ages of two and 12. It offers more than 50 rides, shows, attractions, restaurants, and shops, as well as a botanical garden and a water park. There are also several life-size LEGO displays, along with entertainment options suitable for all ages.

2 Celebration

📍 G2 🏠 E. of I-4 at Exit 25 🌐 celebrationtowncenter.com

Walt Disney conceived of EPCOT® (p26) as a residential community happily road-testing futuristic technologies. After his death,

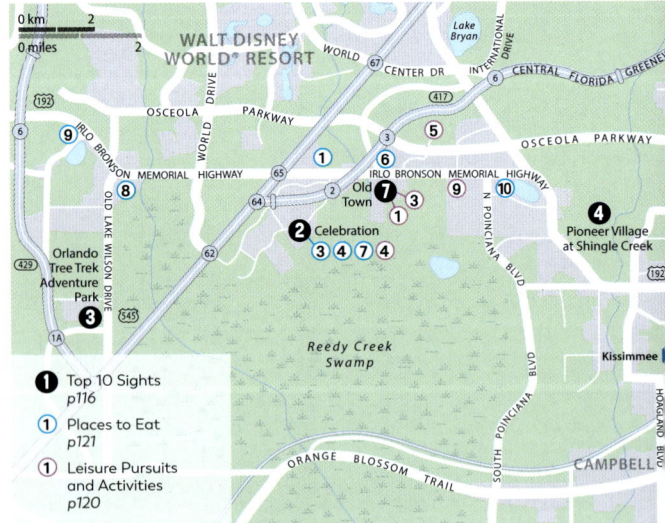

Key:

1 Top 10 Sights
p116

① Places to Eat
p121

① Leisure Pursuits and Activities
p120

For places to stay in this area, see p150

that dream was to resurface years later here. Instead of looking to the future, however, picture-perfect Celebration salutes the past in an upscale cliché of small-town U.S.A., with some good restaurants. This is not an attraction, but it is quite a sight and worth a visit.

3 Orlando Tree Trek Adventure Park

📍 H1 🏠 7625 Sinclair Rd ⏰ 8–11:30am Wed–Fri, 8am–1pm Sat & Sun 🌐 orlandotreetrek.com 🔗

Soar above trees on zip lines, traverse wobbly suspension bridges or swing on Tarzan ropes at this exciting park. Obstacle courses are available to suit all levels.

4 Pioneer Village at Shingle Creek

📍 G3 🏠 2491 Babb Rd ⏰ 10am–4pm daily 🌐 experiencekissimmee.com 🔗

This outdoor museum offers visitors a unique glimpse of Kissimmee life pre-Disney. The focal point here is a pair of beautiful late 1800s

Exhibit on the cattle industry, Pioneer Village

Cracker-style cypress-wood buildings, complete with a cooling "possum trot" breezeway. One of the buildings re-creates a simple home, the other a general store. On sale at this charming store are intriguing local history books, handmade crafts, and handy guides for the nature preserve across the street.

5 Safari Wilderness Ranch

📍 W5 🏠 10850 Moore Rd, Lakeland 🌐 safariwilderness.com 🔗

Want a glimpse into the wilder side of Orlando? Head to this impressive 260-acre (105-ha) family-owned working game ranch, which specializes in cattle and wetland species, such as African Watusi and Irish Dexter. Visitors can soak up stunning open vistas of cypress domes and bay trees with guided tours on a safari vehicle, an ATV, or a kayak. Be sure to check the ranch's website for tour timings.

6 Kennedy Space Center Visitor Complex

The sheer size of this complex (*p52*) makes it a marvel. There are rockets, spacecrafts, and more. Visitors can also opt for shows at the IMAX theaters and explore the world's largest store dedicated to space memorabilia and NASA gear. There are plenty of dining options inside the complex. Guided bus tours around the spaceport are also available.

7 Old Town

📍 G2 🏠 5770 W. Irlo Bronson Memorial Hwy ⏱ 11am–11pm daily 🌐 myoldtownusa.com

Essentially, this is a tourist-oriented shopping mall, which is filled with

Vintage Ford car, Old Town

around 75 stores covering the usual array of gifts, novelty items, and souvenirs – kitsch or otherwise. What sets Old Town apart from other gift-shop strips are the numerous entertainment options: a cheerful 18-ride amusement park, Laser Tag, a Haunted House, carousel, live music performances, and a vintage car show that happens every Friday and Saturday night. It's very much about family fun, and there's no charge for admission, although the carnival rides are priced separately. On a warm Florida night, the feeling is one of strolling the bustling mid-way of a state fair.

8 Silver Spurs Rodeo

📍 H5 🏠 Osceola Heritage Park, 1875 Silver Spur Ln 🌐 silverspursrodeo.com

The largest rodeo east of the Mississippi attracts all the top professional cowboys and is held several times a year. The Silver Spurs Rodeo dates back to 1944 and was from 1950 held in a specially constructed open-air arena, until it was replaced by the state-of-the-art,

Saturn V rocket, Kennedy Space Center Visitor Complex

climate-controlled Silver Spurs Arena in 2002. The arena is also used for concerts and sports events, but will always be chiefly associated with the excitement of the rodeo.

9 Merritt Island

Occupying a vast area, this wildlife reserve *(p48)* is home to endangered species in Florida. Manatees glide in these waters and bird species migrate through these marshlands throughout the year. Explore the area by boat or on foot.

10 Lakefront Park

📍 H4 🏠 1104 Lakefront Blvd, St. Cloud

This park offers a range of amenities, such as pavilions, picnic areas, and playgrounds, and hosts many community events and periodic concerts. There are several miles of pathways for walkers, joggers, skaters, and cyclists, including a sidewalk by Lake Tohopekaliga, which is popular with bird-watchers. It also has a superb white-sand beach, a fishing pier, and an impressive marina. The park has easy access to Kissimmee's historic district, and is close to Chisholm Park and Peghorn Nature Park.

Playing in the splash pad at Lakefront Park

A DAY IN KISSIMMEE

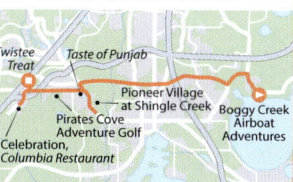

Morning

There are countless breakfast buffets and restaurants in the area. Find the one closest to you and start the day there. As mornings tend to be cooler and a bit less insect-ridden than afternoons, follow your meal with a tour of swamp life with **Boggy Creek Airboat Adventures** *(p120)*. Explore the waterways, then take a walk along the pathways and enjoy the silence broken only by bird calls. For lunch, head to the quaint Disney-designed town of **Celebration**, and pop into **Columbia Restaurant** *(p121)* for sumptuous Cuban cuisine.

Afternoon

From Celebration, it's a 6-mile (9.5-km) drive to **Pioneer Village at Shingle Creek** *(p117)*. Visit the restored dwellings of the earliest settlers in Osceola County on a self-guided tour to see the life of Indigenous peoples. The variety of structures includes a Cracker house, family homes, and a citrus packing house.

Evening

For dinner, head to **Taste of Punjab** *(p121)* for traditional Indian favorites. Afterward, take a short drive to **Pirates Cove Adventure Golf** *(p120)* for a round or two, then head to **Twistee Treat** in Celebration *(twisteetreat. com)* for an ice cream to finish your day.

Leisure Pursuits and Activities

1. Pirates Cove Adventure Golf
G2 2845 Florida Plaza Blvd
piratescove.net
A swashbuckling, tropically landscaped pirate theme has players putt their way through caves and past waterfalls in search of treasure.

2. Bob's Balloon Rides
H1 8293 Championsgate Blvd
bobsballoons.com
Hover high in the sky, taking in the varied landscape – from the lakes and wildlife to the skylines of Central Florida's cities and theme parks.

3. Fun Spot America
G2 2850 Florida Plaza Blvd
10am–midnight daily fun-spot. com
This smaller, family-focused theme park has two popular go-kart tracks and one of the state's few remaining wooden roller coasters, the Mine Blower.

4. Celebration Golf Club
G2 701 Golf Park Dr, Celebration
celebrationgolf.com
Play a challenging round of 18 holes on a course lined by beautiful natural pine forest, set amid the wetlands.

Airboat ride through a swamp at Wild Florida

5. Falcon's Fire Golf Club
G3 3200 Seralago Blvd
falconsfire.com
Immaculately groomed, Falcon's Fire public golf course is said to be one of the best in Florida. It also has exquisite dining facilities.

6. Osceola Arts
H5 2411 E. Irlo Bronson Memorial Hwy osceolaarts.org
Culture mavens will find everything from theater to music events and exhibitions here.

7. Bonanza Golf and Gifts
V3 7761 W. Irlo Bronson Memorial Hwy bonanzagolf. com
Journey back to the Old West at this themed mini-golf spot where you can putt around waterfalls, mines, and sandstone cliffs.

8. Boggy Creek Airboat Adventures
G6 3702 Big Bass Rd
bcairboats.com
These flat-bottomed skiffs with a capacity to carry 18 passengers make regular daytime wildlife trips and special one-hour night tours.

9. Museum of Military History
G3 5210 W. Irlo Bronson Memorial Hwy museumof militaryhistory.com
The interactive exhibits here highlight the American military experience from the Civil War through current conflicts.

10. Wild Florida
W5 Lake Cypress Rd, Kennansville wildfloridaair boats.com
A marvelous safari adventure experience that includes airboat rides through swamps in search of gators and spoonbills, and a drive through a wildlife park and cattle ranch.

Places to Eat

1. Charley's Steak House
G2 2901 Parkway Blvd Lunch
charleyssteakhouse.com · $$$
Charley's uses an Indian cooking method, yielding steaks that are charred outside and juicy inside.

2. Bonefish Grill
G3 2699 W. Osceola Phwy
bonefishgrill.com Lunch · $$
The freshest seafood – including mahi mahi and Chilean sea bass - is prepared on a wood-fired grill.

3. Thai Thani
G2 600 Market St #110,
Celebration thaithanicelebra
tionfl · $$
Immerse yourself in warm and gracious Thai culture at this restaurant known for its extensive and varied menu.

4. Columbia Restaurant
G2 649 Front St, Celebration
columbiarestaurant.com · $$$
Come here for a taste of old Havana. Indulge in crab-stuffed pompano or enjoy the exquisite calamari.

5. El Tapatio Restaurant
H4 1804 W. Vine St eltapatio
kissimmee.com · $$
Meats are marinated overnight in secret signature spices at this popular Mexican joint.

6. Logan's Roadhouse
G2 5925 W. Irlo Bronson
Memorial Hwy logansroad
house.com · $$
BBQ specialties like burgers and ribs are served in a casual setting here.

Entrance to the popular BBQ spot, Logan's Roadhouse

7. Celebration Town Tavern
G2 721 Front St thecelebration
towntavern.com · $$
A quiet gathering spot, which serves great seafood and burgers. Deals on happy hours are available.

8. Black Angus Restaurant
G1 7516 W. Irlo Bronson Memorial Hwy blackangusorlando.com · $$
Succulent steaks are the focus of this award-winning family diner, but ribs and fried chicken are also popular. There's a great breakfast buffet, too.

9. Giordano's Italian Restaurant
G2 7866 W. Irlo Bronson Memorial Hwy giordanos.com · $$
A kid-friendly Italian restaurant, with traditional red-check tablecloths and a menu packed with familiar favorites.

10. Taste of Punjab
G3 4980 W. Irlo Bronson Memorial Hwy tasteofpunjab
orlando.com · $$
A perfect place offering a reasonably priced Indian buffet for both lunch and dinner. A wide range of vegetarian options are on the menu.

DOWNTOWN ORLANDO

Orlando is not just about Walt Disney and theme parks. Long a hub of the banking and citrus-growing industries, Downtown Orlando is also a historic district, and a cultural and natural retreat. It contains several of the city's leading museums, as well as its best-known park, a green oasis surrounding Lake Eola, which offers dramatic skyline vistas. By day Downtown is a relaxed southern enclave, but by night it transforms into an energetic club scene. Orange Avenue is the main street, where herds of partygoers migrate from club to club.

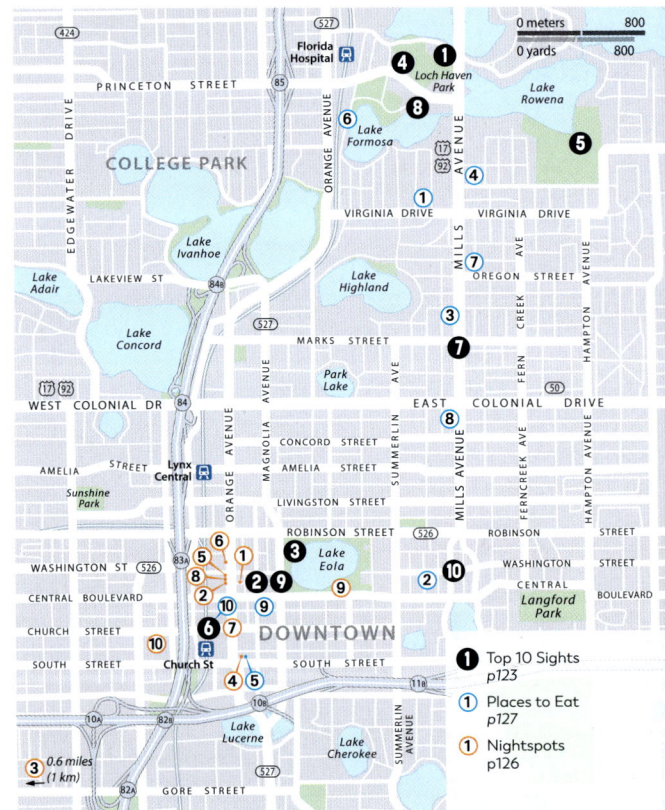

Top 10 Sights
p123

Places to Eat
p127

Nightspots
p126

For places to stay in this area, see p150

Swans on the calm waters of Lake Eola Park

1 Orlando Museum of Art (OMA)

📍 M3 🏛 2416 N. Mills Ave 🕐 10am–4pm Tue–Fri, noon–4pm Sat & Sun 🌐 omart.org ↗

The focus of exhibitions in this big, bright museum is American art from the 19th century onward, art from the ancient Americas and Africa, and blockbuster traveling shows. On the first Thursday evening of every month, you can enjoy music, food, and the work of local artists at an inventively themed get-together.

2 American Ghost Adventures

📍 P3 🏛 Depart from Orange County Regional History Center 🕐 8pm daily 🌐 americanghost adventures.com ↗ ↗

A guide leads visitors through Downtown Orlando, telling tales of the scandals of the city, unsolved mysteries, and hauntings dating back to 1886. The two-hour walk circles back to its starting point, the Orange County Regional History Center, where participants can carry out their own amateur ghost hunt with the help of handheld "ghost detectors."

3 Lake Eola Park

📍 P3

A pedestrian-only path encircles Lake Eola, offering a pleasing view of Downtown's skyline. Those willing to exert their leg muscles can rent swan-shaped paddleboats and take to the water. Real swans drift along in the lake's shallow water and will venture onto dry land if offered a handful of food. Concerts are performed at the Walt Disney Amphitheater, which has surprisingly good acoustics. At night, the landmark illuminated fountain in the middle of the lake produces a light show of changing colors.

4 Orlando Science Center

📍 M3 🏛 777 E. Princeton St 🕐 10am–5pm Thu–Tue 🌐 osc.org ↗

The workings of the natural world, from the infinitesimal to the over-whelming, are on display here. Big interactive fun awaits at the Body Zone, where a huge mouth introduces an exhibit about the digestive system. The vast CineDome shows movies about such topics as ancient Egyptian treasures and ocean life, and on week-end evenings, stargazers can pick out the planets through a telescope.

Canna lily, Harry P. Leu Gardens

5 Harry P. Leu Gardens

📍 N4 🏠 1920 N. Forest Ave 🕐 9am–5pm daily 🌐 leu gardens.org ♿

Well-tended pathways weave through this elegant 50-acre (20-ha) park. Earthy scents waft from a herb garden, while another garden contains plants that attract butterflies. Depending on the season, visitors might catch roses in bloom (in Florida's largest rose garden) or camellias. Guides conduct tours of the early 20th-century Leu House.

6 Church Street

📍 P3 🏠 Between Orange Ave and I-4

The Amway Center has brought life and activity back to Church Street. The influx of restaurants, the renowned theater company Mad Cow Theatre, and the SunRail station have made it even more popular. The Amway Center attracts big-name touring acts, and the stretch of Church Street that lies between Orange Avenue and I-4 has lots of retail stores, restaurants, and bars, keeping visitors amused for hours. The area's original anchor is Church Street Station, a three-level complex constructed around the historic building that was the city's original train station. The complex holds a variety of bars, restaurants, and shops, and it is easy to zigzag between watering holes.

7 The Vietnamese District

📍 N3 🏠 Mills Ave between Virginia Ave and Colonial Dr

This area, also known as the ViMi district (for Virginia and Mills), has been lined with Vietnamese restaurants and shops since the 1970s. You will also find other Asian-owned businesses in this lively district.

8 Mennello Museum of American Art

📍 M3 🏠 900 E. Princeton St 🕐 10:30am–4:30pm Tue–Sat, noon–4:30pm Sun 🌐 mennello museum.com ♿

Half of the Mennello is devoted to the work of Florida folk artist Earl Cunningham (1893–1977), who created vibrant, whimsical pastoral paintings glowing with orange skies and yellow rivers. The other half houses traveling exhibits of folk art. The lakeside grounds contain a scattering of quirky sculptures.

Colorful street-side café on Church Street

Timucua exhibit, Orange County Regional History Center

A DAY DOWNTOWN

Orlando Science Center
White Wolf Cafe
OMA
Mennello Museum of American Art
Little Saigon
Super Rico Colombian Restaurant & Bar
The Social
Orange County Regional History Center
One80 Skytop Lounge
The Bösendorfer Lounge

Morning

Begin with an American breakfast at the **White Wolf Cafe** (p127) before visiting Loch Haven Park, where the **Orlando Science Center** (p123), the **Mennello Museum of American Art**, and the **Orlando Museum of Art (OMA)** (p123) reside within easy walking distance of each other. The Science Center is the best bet for kids. Art lovers can easily hit the Mennello and the OMA in the same morning but if time is short, the OMA deserves priority. Then wander over to **Super Rico Colombian Restaurant & Bar** (superricocolombia.com) for tasty Colombian street food.

Afternoon

After lunch, head to the **Orange County Regional History Center**, which reveals the region's pre-Disney history. Stop at **Little Saigon** (p127) in the Vietnamese district for rice noodle beef soup.

Evening

The Downtown club scene starts late, so kick off with an early cocktail at **The Bösendorfer Lounge** (p126). Fans of live music should head to **The Social** (p126), where shows start around 10pm. The rooftop **One80 Skytop Lounge** (p126) is the perfect spot for cocktails and drinks. Enjoy great views of the city from here.

9 Orange County Regional History Center

 P3 65 E. Central Blvd 10am–5pm Mon–Sat, noon–5pm Sun thehistorycenter.org

From the informative to the kitsch, the Orange County Regional History Center highlights the formative periods and industries of Central Florida. Dioramas show scenes of the early Indigenous people, and there's a re-created Florida Cracker house. A display called "The Day We Changed" chronicles the impact of the arrival of the Disney theme parks – and others that followed. The sinkhole diorama is also intriguing.

10 Thornton Park

 P3

This stylish urban district just east of Lake Eola includes parts of Washington Street, Summerlin Avenue, and Central Boulevard. Thornton Park boasts a number of popular restaurants and bars (among them Dexter's and Eola Wine Company). The area's cobblestone streets are also lined with a number of locally owned shops and boutiques where you can splurge. While a hip neighborhood, Thornton's artisan-style bungalows are one of the area's trademarks.

Partygoers at a nightclub in Wall Street Plaza

Nightspots

1. Wall Street Plaza
P3 26 Wall St wallstplaza.net
This complex features a collection of
bars, clubs, and restaurants – among
them Cantina, the Hen House, Hooch,
Shine, the Monkey Bar, and Waitiki.
Expect a vibrant and loud crowd here.

2. The Beacham
P3 46 N. Orange Ave beacham
orlando.com
This historic building houses a state-
of-the-art nightclub and live music
venue showcasing various genres.

3. Cowboys Orlando
P2 1108 S. Orange Blossom Trail
Sun–Wed cowboysorlando.com
Cowboys is a gigantic country music
hotspot with four huge bars and
nightly dance contests.

4. Bösendorfer Lounge
P3 Grand Bohemian Hotel,
325 S. Orange Ave bosendorfer
lounge.com
An elegant venue perfect for sipping
stylish cocktails. Lounge singers and
pianists perform at the prized
Bösendorfer piano (Fri & Sat).

5. The Social
P3 54 N. Orange Ave the
blockorlando.com
Orlando's best live music club, hosting
an incredible variety of acts, from jazz
to electronica.

6. The Courtesy Bar
P3 114 N. Orange Ave
thecourtesybar.com
A trendy speakeasy bar serving beer,
cocktails, absinthe, and wine. Arrive
early to secure a seat, as it gets busy.

7. Church Street
A two-block strip of bars, clubs, and
restaurants (p124) that draws individ-
uals looking for amusement after a
symphony at the Dr. Phillips Center
(p61) or a game at the Amway Center.

8. Aero Rooftop Bar & Lounge
P3 60 N. Orange Ave
theblockorlando.com/aero
Look out over the skyline of Downtown
Orlando from this Copacabana-styled
rooftop bar. There's a large dance floor
and plenty of space to lounge.

9. Aku Aku Tiki Bar
P3 431 E. Central Blvd
akuakutiki.com
Hawaiian and South Seas kitsch from
the 1940s and 1950s makes for a
unique atmosphere amid the high-
tech Downtown clubs. The bowl-sized
rum punches are highly potent.

10. One80 Skytop Lounge
P2 400 W. Church St
Located in the Amway Center, this
rooftop hotspot offers spectacular
city views. There's VIP seating.
Reservation is recommended.

Places to Eat

1. Santiago's Bodega
N3 802 Virginia Dr
santiagosbodega.com · $
Small tapas plates and house-specialty
sangria are served in a beautiful setting.

2. Graffiti Junktion American Burger Bar
P2 700 E. Washington St
graffitijunhtion.com · $$
A graffiti-covered exterior belies
the great, high-energy burger joint
within. Sunday afternoon karaoke.

3. Tako Cheena
N3 948 N. Mills Ave
tahocheena407.com · $
"Fresh Not Fancy" is the slogan at this
busy restaurant, where Asian fusion
dishes are made to order, with care,
from locally sourced ingredients.

4. Firebirds Wood Fire Grill
N3 1562 N. Mills Ave
firebirdsrestaurants.com · $
A creative menu offers hand-cut
aged steaks, fresh seafood, and
great cocktails at this upscale joint.

5. The Boheme
P3 325 S. Orange Ave
theboheme.com · $$$
Decked with splendid paintings,
this posh restaurant serves game,
steaks, and seafood.

6. White Wolf Cafe
M3 1829 N. Orange Ave
whitewolfcafe.com · $
This eclectic little bistro is known
for its creative menu, painting-filled
interior, and friendly staff.

7. Hawkers Asian Street Food
N3 1103 N. Mills Ave eat
hawkers.com · $
The restaurant serves inviting Asian
street food crafted from recipes
passed down through generations.
Expect bold flavors and a casual vibe.

8. Little Saigon
N3 1106 E. Colonial Dr little
saigonfl.com · $$
Set in the city's thriving Vietnamese
area, this place serves huge bowls
of *pho* (a fragrant and spicy soup
brimming with meat, seafood,
and noodles).

9. Harp & Celt
P3 25 S. Magnolia Ave
harpandceltpub.com · $$
Traditional Irish pub fare is on offer,
along with eclectic daily specials.
Drinks are served at a turn-of-the-
century bar and the outdoor patio
opens when the weather is good.

10. Kres Chophouse
P2 17 W. Church St Sun & lunch
Sat hresrestaurant.com · $$$
Set in a landmark 1930s building, Kres
prides itself on its creative, modern
approach. Feast on local dishes, such
as filet Wellington, or red grouper
from the Florida Keys.

**Lovely frames adorning the
wall at The Boheme**

Clockwise from above
Orlando's dazzling cityscape at dusk; scenic Lake Eola; swan boats for rent on the lake

WINTER PARK, MAITLAND, AND EATONVILLE

True to its name, Winter Park was chartered in 1887 as a winter resort for wealthy – and cold – northerners. Now almost completely surrounded by metropolitan Orlando, it still retains the charm and character of a small, high-end town, with excellent stores and plenty of boutiques, bars, and restaurants, and a sprinkling of interesting museums. The towns of Maitland and Eatonville, to the north and west, are more residential. They have a number of worthwhile attractions, which can make a pleasant change from south Orlando's bustling, commercialized theme parks.

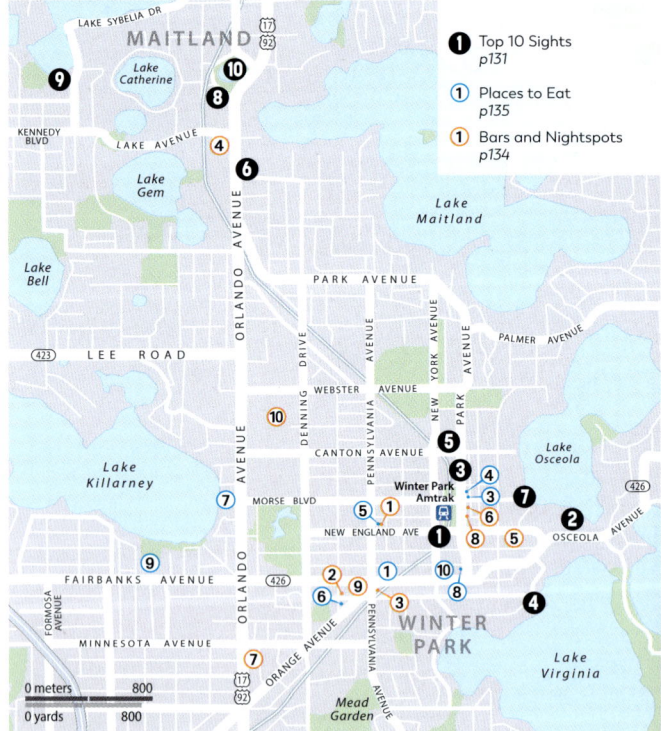

1 Top 10 Sights
p131

1 Places to Eat
p135

1 Bars and Nightspots
p134

For places to stay in this area, see p151

Fresh produce at the Winter Park Farmers' Market

1 Winter Park Farmers' Market

📍 L4 🏠 721 W. New England Ave
🕐 7am–1pm Sat 🌐 cityofwinter
park.org

Some farmers' markets are serious business, packed with old trucks and farmers selling mountains of vegetables just pulled from the earth. The Winter Park Farmers' Market is an altogether different affair. Locals come here to mingle, buy lovely potted flowers, preserves, and fresh herbs, and indulge in delicious croissants, muffins, and breads. There are local vegetables here, too, but this is more of a coffee and brunch gathering.

2 Albin Polasek Museum and Sculpture Gardens

📍 L4 🏠 633 Osceola Ave 🕐 10am–4pm Tue–Sat, 1–4pm Sun 🌐 polasek.org 🔗

Sculptor Albin Polasek moved here to retire from his job, but he kept on producing his figurative works until his death in 1965. Now listed on the National Register of Historic Places, the museum and its sculpture gardens contain works spanning Polasek's entire career.

3 Park Avenue

📍 L4

The stretch of Park Avenue between Fairbanks and Webster avenues is a thriving slice of urban living. There's bucolic Central Park to explore and the low-rise buildings contain fashionable shops and trendy restaurants that will keep you occupied all day long.

4 Rollins Museum of Art

📍 L4 🏠 1000 Holt Ave 🕐 10am–4pm Tue–Fri, noon–5pm Sat & Sun 🌐 rollins.edu/cfam

The art collection at this museum, located on the scenic Rollins College Campus, is one of the oldest in the state. The range of European and American art – dating from the Renaissance to the 20th century – is impeccably presented and of an unusually high quality for a small college art museum.

5 Charles Hosmer Morse Museum of American Art

📍 L4 🏠 445 N. Park Ave 🕐 Hours vary, chech website 🌐 morse museum.org 🔗

This museum contains the world's largest collection of intricate glass windows and objects (including jewelry, leaded-glass lamps, and pottery) by American artist Louis Comfort Tiffany. Other highlights in the museum include an array of ceramics and collections of late 19th- and early 20th-century paintings, graphics, and decorative arts.

Entrance to the charming Enzian Theater

7 Winter Park Scenic Boat Tour

L4 · Morse Blvd at Lake Osceola · scenicboattours.com

The wealthiest sections of Winter Park were built around a series of lakes and along winding canals. This boat tour has been running since 1938, and is part nature trip and part local history lesson. It cruises lazily past Winter Park landmarks and mansions, encountering wildlife, while the skipper tells stories about the legendary society crowd. Tours depart on the hour from 10am to 4pm daily.

6 Enzian Theater

K3 · 1300 S. Orlando Ave · enzian.org

The art of film has a different flavor at the Enzian. This not-for-profit 250-seat theater doesn't just show American independent and foreign films, but also offers a full menu with beer, wine, and table service. Relax with dinner or snacks and enjoy films with all the comforts of your own living room (with the addition of a 33-ft- (10-m-) wide screen). The box office is open every evening from 3pm Monday to Thursday and from noon onward on Friday and weekends. The Enzian is also responsible for the 10-day Florida Film Festival (p90) and puts on festivals all year round.

8 Historic Waterhouse Residence and Carpentry Shop Museum

K3 · 820 Lake Lily Dr · Noon–4pm Thu–Sun · artandhistory.org

William H. Waterhouse was a carpenter who came to Central Florida in the early 1880s and built this lovely home overlooking the beautiful Lake Lily. Pristinely restored and maintained by the Maitland Historical Society, the home, Waterhouse's carpentry shop, and the property's remarkable collection of handcrafted furniture offer a glimpse into Maitland's past. Woodworking buffs will be wowed by Waterhouse's extensive use of heart of pine, a wood rarely seen today. Tours lasting about 40 minutes are offered. The Waterhouse facilities

The tranquil greenery of Lake Lily Park

complement the Maitland Historical Museum, Maitland Art Center, and Telephone Museum *(p59)*, all just a few blocks away and also run by the Maitland Historical Society.

9 Audubon Center for Birds of Prey

📍 K3 🏠 1101 Audubon Way 🕐 10am–4pm Tue–Sun 🌐 audubonofflorida.org ⬈

Think of this place as a halfway house for some of Florida's most impressive birds. It was created by the Florida Audubon Society to rescue, rehabilitate, and release wounded raptors (birds of prey). Those that wouldn't survive being released into the wild are kept here, living a pampered existence in a lovely lakeside location, while helping to educate visitors about wildlife issues and conservation. Visitors aren't allowed to observe the rehabilitation process itself, but permanent residents on view usually include vultures, bald eagles, screech owls, hawks, ospreys, and more.

10 Lake Lily Park

📍 K3 🏠 701 Lake Lily Dr, Maitland 🌐 itsmymaitland.com

This park is made up of 5 acres (2 ha) of lush landscaping around Lake Lily, offering visitors plenty of secluded, shady areas for picnics. There's also a quiet boardwalk that winds beside the lake, jogging trails, and the restored Waterhouse Residence Museum.

A DAY IN WINTER PARK

Morning

Begin with a hearty breakfast at the **Briarpatch Restaurant** *(thebriarpatchrestaurant.com)*. Afterward, wander the north end of **Park Avenue** *(p131)*, where one-off boutiques cater to upscale shopping tastes. At Canton Avenue, pop in to the **Charles Hosmer Morse Museum of American Art** *(p131)*; its outstanding collection of Tiffany glass is a must-see. Follow this with a relaxing trip on the **Winter Park Scenic Boat Tour**, which departs from a dock on Morse Boulevard, just a 15-minute walk away. On your return, lunch options are plentiful along Park Avenue. Choose the one that most takes your fancy and tuck into some good food.

Afternoon

After lunch, continue south on Park Avenue to Rollins College, home of the excellent **Rollins Museum of Art**, and spend the rest of the afternoon enjoying this small but wonderful collection.

Evening

It's a 10-minute car ride north to Maitland's **Enzian Theater**, where you can enjoy the latest in independent films with a bottle of wine and a cheese plate. End the day with a lakeside meal at **Hillstone** *(p135)*, just a few minutes south by car.

Bars and Nightspots

1. Hannibal's on the Square
📍 L4 🏠 511 W. New England Ave
🌐 hannibalslounge.com
Part café, part casual upscale bar, Hannibal's shares seating space with a tremendous French restaurant.

2. Forward Slash Distillery
📍 L4 🏠 650 S. Capen Ave
🌐 drinkforwardslash.com
Spirits and cocktail lovers can sample rye whiskey, gin, rum, and bourbon distilled on the premises. The liquor flights and tasting classes are popular.

3. Fiddler's Green
📍 L4 🏠 544 W. Fairbanks Ave
🌐 fiddlersgreen.pub
This energetic Irish pub with good food has darts, music, and a selection of draft beers and stouts.

4. Copper Rocket Pub
📍 K3 🏠 106 Lake Ave
🌐 thecopperrocket.com
With its small stage hosting anything from jazz jams to psychedelia, this is the only real music bar in the area.

5. Hamilton's Kitchen
📍 L4 🏠 Alfond Inn, 300 E. New England Ave 🌐 hamiltonshit chen.com
A classy cocktail haven in a chic hotel with a go-to Sunday brunch.

Outdoor seating at Hannibal's on the Square

6. The Parkview
📍 L4 🏠 136 Park Ave
🌐 theparkviewwp.com
An extensive menu of wines by the glass is on offer at this wine shop and bar. Drinks are complemented by a wide range of snacks and desserts.

7. Marlow's Tavern
📍 L3 🏠 1008 S. Orlando Ave
🌐 marlowstavern.com
Black-and-white photos adorn brick walls of this modern tavern. Fill up on gourmet flatbreads, salads, and burgers, or more substantial fare.

8. The Wine Room
📍 L4 🏠 270 S. Park Ave
🌐 thewineroomonline.com
Wine is showcased here, with over 156 bottles hand-selected for sampling. There is also a selection of artisan cheeses and a tapas-style menu.

9. The Porch
📍 L4 🏠 643 Orange Ave 🗓 Mon
🌐 theporchsouthorange.com
A menu featuring burgers and wings and other home-style favorites is accompanied by a comprehensive list of cocktails and beers here.

10. Flûtes Champagne Bar
📍 L3 🏠 480 N. Orlando Ave, Suite 133
🌐 fluteschampagnebar.com
This elegant champagne bar is one of the more refined, upscale spots in the area.

Places to Eat

1. Ravenous Pig
⚲ L4 **⌂** 565 W. Fairbanks Ave
Ⓦ theravenouspig.com · **$$$**
Local, organic, and Southern food by James Beard-nominated chefs is served alongside a wide choice of drinks.

2. Christner's Prime Steak & Lobster
⚲ K2 **⌂** 729 Lee Rd **Ⓦ** christnersprime steahandlobster.com · **$$$**
At this family-owned restaurant, locally sourced ingredients are used, along with imported cold-water lobster and the best cuts of beef.

3. Bosphorous Turkish Cuisine
⚲ L4 **⌂** 108 S. Park Ave **Ⓦ** bosphorous restaurant.com · **$$**
Treat your tastebuds with classics, such as moussaka and babaganoush, at this spot. There's no kids' menu, though.

4. Prato
⚲ L4 **⌂** 124 W. Park Ave **⌚** Lunch Mon & Tue **Ⓦ** prato-wp.com · **$$$**
Enjoy outdoor seating at this restaurant that offers classic Italian cuisine.

5. Mynt Fine Indian Cuisine
⚲ L4 **⌂** 535 W. New England Ave
Ⓦ myntorlando.com · **$$**
Indulge in a traditional Indian feast, inspired by a variety of culinary influences. There are plenty of meat-free dishes, too.

6. Winter Park Fish Company
⚲ L4 **⌂** 761 Orange Ave **⌚** Sun
Ⓦ wpfishco.com · **$$**
This family-owned counter-service spot serves dinner on picnic tables. First

Whole squid served with *yuzu kosho* aioli at Umi

pick your fish, then choose how you want it prepared, add a topping, and pick two sides.

7. Hillstone
⚲ L3 **⌂** 215 S. Orlando Ave
Ⓦ hillstonerestaurant.com · **$$**
Locals often come to witness the sunset over the lake at this lovely restaurant. Portions are huge and seafood options are also available.

8. Umi
⚲ L4 **⌂** 525 S. Park Ave
Ⓦ umiwinterpark.com · **$$**
Japanese fusion cuisine with a side of sushi is what you'll find on the menu here. Plates are served tapas-style, allowing everyone to share the dishes.

9. 4 Rivers Smokehouse
⚲ L4 **⌂** 1600 W. Fairbanks Ave
Ⓦ 4rsmokehouse.com · **$$**
The award-winning modern barbecue served here features plenty of options. Be sure not to miss the red velvet cake and other decadent desserts.

10. The Hen and Hog
⚲ L4 **⌂** 221 W. Fairbanks Ave · **$$**
Food is served with a rustic twist here, like the namesake sandwich, which puts chicken and pulled pork on a ciabatta roll. Expect casual southern classics.

STREETSMART

Getting Around   134   138

Practical Information   142

Theme Park Tips   146

Places to Stay   148

Index   152

Acknowledgments   158

Signs at Universal CityWalk™

GETTING AROUND

Whether exploring Orlando by foot or making use of public transportation, here is everything you need to know to navigate the city and the areas beyond the center like a pro.

Arriving by Air

Three airports serve Orlando: **Orlando International Airport**, **Orlando Sanford International Airport**, and the private Orlando Executive Airport.

Orlando International Airport is the city's busiest airport, handling the majority of national and international flights. It is located 12 miles (20 km) southeast of the city center. There are taxis, shuttle services, hotel shuttles, and rental cars located at ground level, below the arrival area. Public transportation, via the LYNX bus, is also available; however, service is limited to two stops located in the city and two stops along International Drive.

Orlando Sanford International Airport is located 23 miles (37 km) northeast of the city center and 48 miles (77 km) from the major tourist districts. Taxis, private shuttles, and rental cars are available for hire, but there is no public transportation.

Be sure to allow plenty of extra time at the airport, both at arrival and departure, as there are often long lines.
Orlando International Airport
🅦 orlandoairports.net
Orlando Sanford International Airport
🅦 flysfb.com

Train Travel

Amtrak, the national passenger rail company, serves Florida from the east coast. There is one daily service from New York City. This Silver Service takes up to 28 hours (with sleepers and meals available), and runs via Washington D.C., down through Orlando. The Palmetto serves the same route and offers a business-class service. When traveling overnight, you can choose between the seats of coach class or a cabin. Both options have decent meal services on longer stretches.

If you want to travel by train to Florida but take your own car to drive once you get there, book a ticket on

Amtrak's Auto Train, which runs daily from Lorton in Virginia to Sanford, Florida – 30 miles (48 km) north of Orlando. The journey takes 18 hours.

Amtrak trains serve a limited number of cities in Florida. Other than Tampa, the Gulf Coast is linked only by Amtrak buses, known as "Thruway" buses. These run from Winter Haven, near Orlando, to Fort Myers via St. Petersburg and Sarasota, with guaranteed connections with rail services.

In 2023, **Brightline** launched a train connection between Orlando and Miami; the high-speed train takes three and a half hours.

Amtrak
W amtrak.com
Brightline
W gobrightline.com

Long-Distance Bus Travel
Greyhound buses offer the cheapest way to get around Florida. To reserve in advance visit the Greyhound website. You can also go to a Greyhound agent – usually found in a local store or post office – or pay the driver directly.

Passes provide unlimited travel for set periods of time (between four and 60 days), but you may only find them useful if you have a very full itinerary.

Red Coach runs smaller, premium buses – offering movies, Wi-Fi, and reclining seats – from Miami to Orlando.
Greyhound
W greyhound.com
Red Coach
W redcoachusa.com

Public Transportation
Orlando has a good public transportation network which includes trains and buses. Safety and hygiene measures, timetables, ticket information,

and transport maps can be obtained at tourist information centers, stations, and individual operators' websites.

Trains
The **SunRail** commuter train connects stations running from the north to Kissimmee through Downtown Orlando, Winter Park, Sanford, and across the St. Johns to DeBary. The service runs on weekdays until 9pm, and sporadically on the weekend.
SunRail
W sunrail.com

Buses and Trolleys
You can get by in Orlando without a car thanks to the local **LYNX** buses, which serve the main tourist areas of Downtown Orlando, International Drive, and Walt Disney World® Resort. The free **Lymmo** service (run by LYNX) travels within Downtown Orlando, with rides to and from the Amway Center sports arena.

Tickets can be purchased online or at a number of Ace Cash Express locations throughout the area. If paying when boarding the bus, make sure that you have cash. It is recommended that you pay with the exact fare, as drivers can't always provide change.

The **I-Ride Trolley** provides hop-on/hop-off transportation that runs the length of International Drive and Universal Blvd (both on the green line). Trolleys run every 20–30 minutes, operating between 8:30am and 10pm. Pay as you board the trolley, or go online to buy passes for up to 14 days.
I-Ride Trolley
W internationaldriveorlando.com/iride-trolley
LYNX and Lymmo
W golynx.com

GETTING TO AND FROM THE AIRPORT

Airport	Destination	Distance	Taxi Fare
Orlando International Airport	Downtown Orlando	12 miles (20 km)	$40
	Universal Studios Florida™	15 miles (24 km)	$40–60
	Magic Kingdom® Park	18 miles (28 km)	$70

Taxis

Taxis are a comfortable though expensive way of getting around. Due to the popularity of ride-hailing services like Uber, taxicabs are becoming increasingly scarce, though you can still hail a taxi in front of most hotels, resorts, at major attractions, and at the airport. Most have a "TAXI" sign on the roof; this is illuminated if the taxi is free.

You can also call for taxi services such as **Star Taxi** and **Mears Taxi Yellow**. Expect the meter to start at around $3.25 for the first mile, then add a charge of $2 or more per mile after that.

Mears Taxi Yellow
📞 407-422-2222
Star Taxi
📞 407-857-9999

Driving in Orlando

Driving in Florida is, by and large, an efficient way to get around urban areas and travel between cities. It's also very straightforward: most highways are well-paved, gasoline is relatively inexpensive, and car rental rates are the lowest in the US.

The sheer volume of traffic in the main tourist areas of Orlando can pose some challenges for drivers. Traffic is heavy along I-4, U.S. 192, 535, and 536. The busiest times are early in the morning, during the early evening, and late at night. The main toll roads are BeachLine Expressway (between Orlando and the Space Coast) and the Florida Turnpike, which runs from I-75 northwest of Orlando to Florida City. The toll you have to pay depends on the distance covered. Tolls can be paid to a collector in a booth or – if you have the correct change and do not need a receipt – dropped into a collecting bin.

There are several toll roads in Florida that feature all-electronic tolling. Note that most sections of the Turnpike have been converted to an electronic collection system and cash is no longer used. Tolls are collected via Sunpass transponders or from having your license plate photographed at each toll booth.

Take care when approaching exits, which can be on both sides of the highway; most accidents occur when making left turns.

Finding a parking space is rarely a problem at theme parks and other major tourist attractions, shopping malls, or in most downtown districts. Parking near beaches is more difficult. Note that parking at Walt Disney World® Resort hotels for registered guests is not complimentary, and prices range from $15 to $25 per vehicle per night.

Car Rental

Most visitors arrive by air and rent a car to get around. Rental companies include **Alamo**, **Avis**, **Budget**, and **National**; these businesses are located at the airports, as well as at a small number of larger hotels. It is usually cheaper to rent a vehicle at the airport rather than from a downtown outlet.

To rent a car in Orlando, you are required to have a valid driver's license and (for international travelers only) a passport. Credit cards are the only form of payment accepted – no debit cards. The minimum age for car rental is 21, but drivers under 25 may need to pay a surcharge. The state of Florida requires that you carry a copy of the rental agreement in the car. It is recommended to store it safely out of sight.

When renting a car, make sure your rental agreement includes Collision Damage Waiver (CDW) – also known as Loss Damage Waiver (LDW) – or you'll be liable for any damage to the car, even if it was not your fault. Rental agreements include third-party insurance, but this is rarely adequate. It is advisable to buy additional liability insurance, in the event that something unexpected happens.

Most companies add a premium if you want to drop the car off in another city, and all impose high charges for gas: if you return the car with less fuel than it had initially, you will be required to pay the inflated fuel prices charged by the rental agencies. Be aware that the gas stations nearest airports are particularly expensive.

Alamo
W alamo.com

Avis
W avis.com

Budget
W budget.com

National
W national.com

Rules of the Road
While there are many state and federal regulations on the equipment require-ments of cars, there are very few that pertain to occupants. There is no requirement to carry warning triangles or safety flares, for instance. Drivers and passengers can be fined for not wearing seatbelts, and at certain times of the year state-wide campaigns make violations particularly expensive; heavy fines can be levied at checkpoints by the Florida Highway Patrol. Children under three must sit in a child seat.

Drinking and driving is illegal. Driv-ing under the influence can result in a fine, having your driver's license sus-pended, or imprisonment.

Drive on the right-hand side of the road. Passing is allowed on both sides on any multilane road, including inter-state highways. It is illegal to change lanes across a double yellow or double white solid line. If a school bus stops on a two-way road to drop off or pick up children, traffic traveling in both directions must stop. On a divided highway, only traffic traveling in the same direction need stop.

Cycling
Cycling is a fun alternative to walking around the city, and the area is filled with bike paths. Rentals are available at a number of locations for recre-ational use, including **West Orange Trail Bikes & Blades**. In the city cen-ter, **HOPR Bike Share** allows you to reserve a bike online or via your smartphone, pick it up at any of the

citywide locations (some found north of the city), then simply return it to one of the authorized racks.

HOPR Bike Share
W gohopr.com/orlando

West Orange Trail Bikes & Blades
W orlandobikerental.com

Walking
The city center is easily explored by foot. However, it can be uncomfortable in Orlando's hot and humid summer weather. The theme parks also have walkable areas, but travel between hotels and attractions is best achieved by a vehicle.

Away from the center, Orlando has been ranked as one of the most dangerous cities for pedestrians, due to the wide highways and a lack of sidewalks, crosswalks, and streetlights. It is advisable to use public transpor-tation or a rental car to get around.

Theme Park Transportation
The theme parks and hotels at Walt Disney World® Resort are up to 6 miles (11 km) apart, with little or no desig-nated walking paths. Traveling is kept simple as Disney operates several modes of transportation that go to guest areas, including buses, mono-rails, boats, and the Skyliner gondolas.

The bus system links every on-site hotel, the four major theme parks, water parks, and Disney Springs™. It runs 45 mins prior to park opening until two hours after closing.

Water taxis and ferries operate between select on-site resorts and theme parks, while the monorail – the quickest mode of transportation – links the Magic Kingdom® to a handful of Disney's hotels, EPCOT®, and the Ticket and Transportation area.

Universal Orlando Resort™ runs buses between the on-site hotels and theme parks. There is also a water-taxi service between CityWalk™, the Hard Rock Hotel, Royal Pacific Hotel, and Portofino Bay Hotel. Transportation is free for guests.

PRACTICAL INFORMATION

A little local know-how goes a long way in Orlando. On these pages you can find all the essential advice and information you will need to make the most of your trip to this city.

AT A GLANCE

CURRENCY
Dollar (USD)

AVERAGE DAILY SPEND

SAVE	SPEND	SPLURGE
$160	$220	$350

BOTTLED WATER	COFFEE	BEER	DINNER FOR TWO
$3.50	$5	$9	$100

CLIMATE

Summers are long, hot, and fairly humid. Temperatures in July hit 82°F (28°C).

Winters are mild. Temperatures can sink to 61°F (16°C) in January.

Short, sharp downpours are the norm in the wet season (May–Sep). Hurricane season is from June to November.

ELECTRICITY SUPPLY
The standard U.S. electric current is 110 volts and 60 Hz. Power sockets are type A and B, fitting plugs with two flat pins.

Passports and Visas
For entry requirements, including visas, consult your nearest U.S. embassy or check with the **U.S. State Department**.
    Canadian visitors just require a valid passport to enter the U.S. Citizens of Australia, New Zealand, the UK, and the EU do not need a visa, but must apply to enter in advance via the Electronic System for Travel Authorization (**ESTA**) and have a valid passport. Visitors from all other regions will require a tourist visa and passport to enter. A return airline ticket is required to enter the country.
ESTA
W esta.cbp.dhs.goc/esta
U.S. State Department
W travel.state.gov

Government Advice
Now more than ever, it is important to consult both your and the U.S. government's advice before traveling. The U.S. State Department, **UK Foreign, Commonwealth and Development Office** (FCDO), and the **Australian Department of Foreign Affairs and Trade** offer the latest information on security, health and local regulations.
Australian Department of Foreign Affairs and Trade
W smartraveller.gov.au
UK Foreign, Commonwealth and Development Office
W gov.uk/foreign-travel-advice

Customs Information
You can find information on the laws relating to goods and currency taken in or out of the U.S. on the **Customs and Border Protection Agency** website. All travelers need to complete a Customs and Border Protection Agency form.
U.S. Customs and Border Protection
W cbp.gov

Insurance
We recommend that you take out a comprehensive insurance policy

covering theft, loss of belongings, medical care, cancelations and delays, and read the small print carefully.

All medical treatment is private and U.S. health insurers do not have reciprocal arrangements with other countries so it is important to take out comprehensive medical insurance.

Vaccinations

No inoculations are required to visit the U.S.

Money

Most establishments accept major credit, debit, and prepaid currency cards, and contactless payments are widespread. It is still worth carrying cash for smaller shops and restaurants.

Tipping is an important custom in Florida. Anyone who provides a service expects to receive a "gratuity." Waiters and taxi drivers will expect to be tipped 15 per cent of the total bill, while hotel porters and housekeeping should be given $5 per bag or day.

Travelers With Specific Requirements

U.S. federal laws require that all public establishments provide accessible entrances and other facilities for those with specific requirements.

Public buses, along with Disney and Universal buses, have hydraulic lifts and restraining belts for wheelchairs, and some buses have "kneeling" wheelchair access – look for a sticker on the windshield or by the door. The Disney monorail and select water-craft traveling between the theme parks and resorts are also equipped for wheelchairs. A few car rental companies, including **Wheelchair Gateways**, have vehicles adapted for people with disabilities. Special park guides outline all of the services available to guests with specific requirements while at the theme parks, including special parking and assisted listening devices.

Outside of the parks, a number of groups offer general advice for travelers with specific requirements, including **Mobility International U.S.A.** and **Visit Florida**. **Lighthouse Central Florida** is a useful resource for visually impaired travelers and **Florida Disabled Outdoors Association** lists recreational activities throughout the state.

Florida Disabled Outdoors Association
W fdoa.org
Lighthouse Central Florida
W lighthousecfl.org
Mobility International U.S.A.
W miusa.org
Visit Florida
W visitflorida.com
Wheelchair Gateways
W wheelchairgetaways.com

Language

English is the official language in the U.S.; however, large Hispanic and Latin American communities mean Spanish is widely spoken in many areas around Orlando.

Opening Hours

Office hours are generally from 9am to 6pm Monday through Friday. Some businesses, such as shops and malls, are open from 10am to 9pm Monday through Saturday and 11am to 7pm Sunday.

Banks are generally open from 8am to 4pm on weekdays; some are open Saturdays 9am to noon (and sometimes to 2pm).

Attractions and theme parks have their own operating hours that change seasonally – and sometimes weekly or even daily. It is best to check each individual website for the most up-to-date information.

Situations can change quickly and unexpectedly. Always check before visiting attractions and hospitality venues for up-to-date opening hours and booking requirements.

Personal Security

Orlando is a relatively safe city, but as with any city, it is still advisable to take precautions. Be alert to pickpockets, particularly in crowded amusement parks. At night, avoid badly lit areas (especially Downtown's westside, south of Colonial Drive).

AT A GLANCE

EMERGENCY NUMBERS

GENERAL EMERGENCY

911

TIME ZONE
EST (Eastern Standard Time), except for Panhandle – CST (Central Standard Time).

TAP WATER
Unless otherwise stated, tap water in Florida is safe to drink.

WEBSITES

visitorlando.com
The city's tourist board
visitflorida.com
Florida's state tourist board
nhc.noaa.gov
National Hurricane Center
ready.gov/hurricanes
Lists safety precautions in the event of a hurricane
amtrak.com
The U.S. rail network
greyhound.com
America's national bus network

Lockers are located at most of the major attractions and are a safe place to store your valuables while exploring the theme parks. Expect to have your bags inspected as you enter any of the major attractions in the area.

Report all lost or stolen items to the police, and make sure you get a copy of the police report for your insurance claim at home. If your passport goes missing, you must contact the embassy of your home country immediately. If you need emergency services, dial the countrywide emergency number 911.

As a rule, Floridians are accepting of all people, regardless of their race, gender or sexuality. The state has a large Latin American and African American population. Following the Black Lives Matter protests sparked by the killing of George Floyd in the summer of 2020, some confederate statues have been removed, and buildings and squares named after historical figures have been renamed.

Florida has a long history as an LGBTQ+-friendly vacation destination, and Orlando has long supported the community. There is a vibrant LGBTQ+ nightlife scene, and the city has been hosting its annual Pride parade since 1991. This attitude, however, does not always extend to the state's more rural areas. If you do feel unsafe while in the city, or when taking day trips out of Orlando, the **Safe Space Alliance** pinpoints your nearest place of refuge.

Florida is occasionally at risk from hurricanes (from June to November); advance warnings are activated if there is any danger.

Emergency Services
📞 911
Safe Space Alliance
🌐 safespacealliance.com

Health

The U.S. does not have a government health program, so emergency medical and dental care, though excellent, can be very expensive. Payment of hospital and other medical expenses is the patient's responsibility, as such it is always important to arrange comprehensive medical insurance before you travel. Keep receipts to make a claim on your insurance.

For less serious complaints, many drugstores such as Walgreens and CVS (some of which stay open late or for 24 hours) have registered clinics. For more serious medical ailments, there are several walk-in care clinics where no appointment is necessary, including **Lake Buena Vista Centra Care**. The city's major hospitals are the **Advent Health** and the **Orlando Regional Medical Center**. If you become ill or hurt while in the theme parks, first-aid stations can provide assistance.

Advent Health
🔳 adventhealth.com/hospital/adventhealth-orlando
Lake Buena Vista Centra Care
📞 407-934-2273
Orlando Regional Medical Center
📞 321-841-5111

Smoking, Alcohol, and Drugs
Florida has a partial smoking ban, with lighting up prohibited in most enclosed spaces and on public transportation. E-cigarettes have the same rules.

You must be over 21 to buy and drink alcohol, and to buy tobacco products. It is advisable to carry valid ID at all times, as you will not be permitted to enter bars or order alcoholic beverages in restaurants without ID.

The possession of narcotics is strictly prohibited and could result in prosecution and a prison sentence.

ID
There is no requirement for visitors to carry ID, but due to occasional checks (especially at Federal sites) you may be asked to show a picture ID. When driving, you must carry your license with you at all times.

Responsible Tourism
Orlando is a leading city in the U.S. for sustainability and green living, with the city championing renewable energy and encouraging eco-friendly initiatives. Orlando's big theme parks also do their part – Universal Studios Florida™ recycles around 10,000 tons of food waste and recyclable materials annually, while Walt Disney World® Resort has over 500,000 solar panels to help power its parks.

There are simple ways visitors can help toward the city's sustainable future. Reduce emissions by cycling or walking around Downtown Orlando, use reusable water bottles and bags when out and about, and embrace the array of locally and sustainably sourced cuisine.

Cell Phones and Wi-Fi
Orlando International Airport, along with most hotels and restaurants, offers Wi-Fi or high-speed Internet access. While some places offer access free of charge, many hotels charge a fee of at least $9.99 to use the service for a 24-hour period.

Cell phone service is excellent. If you are coming from overseas and want to ensure that your cell phone will work, get a quad-band phone. The "roaming" facility is expensive, but if you are using your phone for Wi-Fi, data roaming can be turned off. Other options include buying a prepaid cell phone in the U.S. or a SIM chip for a U.S. carrier.

Post
Main branches of the U.S. Post Office are usually open from 8am to 4pm Monday through Friday and 8am to 1pm Saturdays, with select branches open extended hours. Stamped letters and postcards may be dropped off at the front desk of most hotels. Stamps for a first-class letter cost 49 cents.

Taxes and Refunds
The state sales tax in Florida is 6 per cent. Local authorities can add additional levies up to a maximum 2.5 per cent; Orlando's tax rate is 6.5 per cent.

THEME PARK TIPS

Beat the Crowds

Theme park crowds are thinnest from the second week in September to the third week in November, the first two weeks of December, mid-January to mid-March, and late April through the third week of May. Weekends are always busy.

Tickets

Buy tickets online for **Walt Disney World®** to save time waiting in line; they must be picked up in person. For **Universal Orlando Resort™** print out tickets at home, or collect them from the gate for an extra $2.50 per ticket. Tickets for LEOGLAND® are considerably cheaper to purchase online in advance; they can then be printed out at home.

LEGOLAND®

Ⓦ legoland.com/florida/tickets-passes/tickets

Universal Orlando Resort™

Ⓦ universalorlando.com/Theme-Park-Tickets/General-Admission.aspx

Walt Disney World®

Ⓦ disneyworld.disney.go.com/tickets

Multiday and Multipark Passes

Disney's Park Hopper and Park Hopper Plus tickets are valid for four to seven days. Both include unlimited entry to the four parks; the Park Hopper Plus tickets also include entry to other Disney attractions. The discounts aren't great, but you will save time waiting in line. Universal Studios Florida™, Universal's Islands of Adventure™, Wet 'n Wild®, SeaWorld® Orlando, Aquatica® Water Park, and Busch Gardens® Tampa Bay offer the unlimited-access, 14-day FlexTicket.

Arrival Times

Most theme park attractions open to the public at 9am. Although it may seem sensible to hit the parks as soon as they open and avoid the lines, this is rarely a good idea if you are traveling with small children, as kids who arrive early tend to be exhausted by 2pm. Instead, take it easy in the morning and head for the parks in late afternoon and evenings. Temperatures are usually cooler, too.

Cutting Time in Line

Universal and SeaWorld® (Express™ Pass) offer a system that cuts out the long wait for the most popular rides and shows. Just slide your ticket through the turnstile to get an allocated spot for your visit. When it's time, simply go to the particular attraction's designated entrance to take your place.

Stroller Rental and Baby Care

All the major theme parks offer stroller rental. There are also excellent nursing facilities, often with free formula provided. Diaper-changing tables can also be found in women's and some men's restrooms.

Getting Wet

Take a change of clothes to the theme parks – especially if you are traveling with kids. Apart from water rides where you might expect to get wet, kids enjoy running through "splash areas" to cool off. A rain poncho is smart year-round and is worth buying before you get to the parks.

Breaks

Theme parks are tiring at any time of the year but excessively so in summer, when even standing in line can be exhausting. Plan regular breaks at air-conditioned venues or "splash areas," particularly around midday, when the outside temperatures are at their hottest.

Snacks and Water

Theme park prices for refreshments are 30–50 per cent higher than you will find outside. The parks prohibit coolers (containers for keeping food and drink cool), but guests can bring bottled water and snacks. There are also a few water fountains dotted around the parks.

Many restaurants at Walt Disney World® accept reservations 120 days in advance, and guests are recommended to book well ahead, especially for unique experiences such as character dining.

Ride Restrictions

Disney parks tend to have few health and height restrictions, although Disney Hollywood Studios® is a little limiting. Universal's parks can be more restrictive for younger kids, especially Universal's Islands of Adventure™ (where there are warnings on most of the major rides), but like Universal Studios Florida™, it does have a dedicated kids' area. LEGOLAND® has height restrictions on some of its rides.

Parent-Swaps

Height restrictions mean that younger children may not be able to go on certain rides. The theme parks usually have a program that lets one parent ride while the other tends to the kids in a special waiting area; then the second parent can go on the ride without having to wait in line again.

Name Tags and Reunion Places

It's very easy to get lost in crowded theme parks. If that happens, find a park employee (they're usually in uniform), and ask for help. Kids aged seven and under should wear tags bearing their name, hotel, and a contact number. Older children and adults should pick a place inside the park to meet if they become separated.

VIP Tours

VIP tours at both **Walt Disney World Resort®** and **Universal Orlando Resort™** take guests on a relatively customized whirlwind tour of the parks. Included is front-row seating for shows, front-of-the-line access to rides and attractions, and your very own tour guide. At Universal, breakfast and lunch, bottled water, and parking are all included; however, the itinerary is slightly less flexible, with a set start and length.

Disney adds door-to-door transportation (picking you up and dropping you back off at your hotel) and a flexible start time, with the ability to add extra time, but no meals are included. Enjoying personalized attention and behind-the-scenes access comes at a price, though, with Disney VIP tours running $400–600 per hour for up to ten guests, with a six-hour minimum, depending on the season, while Universal prices start at $189 per person for group tours, with private-tour costs starting at approximately $1,200.

Universal Orlando Resort™
🅦 universalorlando.com/Theme-Park-Tickets/VIP-Experience.aspx
Walt Disney World Resort®
🅦 disneyworld.disney.go.com/events-tours/vip-tour-services

Behind-the-Scenes Tours

Walt Disney World® offers a whole host of behind-the-scenes tours. Disney's Backstage Magic is a seven-hour tour that showcases the inner workings of all four theme parks (including the technology behind EPCOT®, the underground operations of Magic Kingdom®, and more). Keys to the Kingdom is a five-hour taster tour for guests who would like to see what's on offer before they really get started; it provides a basic park orientation, as well as a glimpse of some of the usually hidden high-tech magic. The Family Magic Tour is a great choice if you have kids along, offering a two-hour scavenger hunt through Disney's most child-friendly park, the Magic Kingdom®.

Walt Disney World®
🅦 disneyworld.disney.go.com/events-tours

PLACES TO STAY

Outside of a few boutique options downtown, Orlando's hotels are branded, themed extensions of the parks, with resort-style facilities (and prices to match). Hotels beyond the theme parks offer perks such as shuttle buses to the main attractions.

Family vacations in summer and the December holidays drive the tourist seasons, with cheaper deals January–February and September–November. Room rates are usually quoted without hotel tax, which is 6 percent in the Orlando area.

PRICE CATEGORIES

For a standard double room per night (with breakfast if included), including taxes and extra charges.

$ under $180
$$ $180–$250
$$$ over $250

Walt Disney World® Resort and Lake Buena Vista

Hilton Orlando Lake Buena Vista – Disney Springs® Area

📍X2 🏠1751 Hotel Plaza Blvd, Lake Buena Vista 🌐hilton.com · $$

A perfect option for those who want to spend their holiday immersed in the magic of Disney, this Hilton property is set on a vast swath of landscaped land with lakeside views of Disney Springs®. When not enjoying the rides and experiences at the parks (accessible via free shuttle bus), relax in one of the two outdoor pools or enjoy the arcade.

Disney's Grand Floridian Resort and Spa

📍V1 🏠 4401 Floridian Way, Lake Buena Vista 🌐disneyworld.disney. go.com · $$$

Imagine watching the fireworks light up over Cinderella's Castle from the comfort of your room.

At Disney's flagship property, dreams become reality. This resort overlooks the spectacular Magic Kingdom®, putting you in prime position for everything the park has to offer.

Conrad Orlando

📍X1 🏠 1500 Eastbeach Way 🌐hilton.com · $$$

Looking to escape the theme parks? Lose yourself in 1,100 acres (440 ha) of water gardens, lagoons, and a sprawling golf course at this lovely hotel. For those looking to escape the Floridian sun, too, the on-site spa achieves the usual Conrad standards.

Four Seasons Resort Orlando

📍W1 🏠10100 Dream Tree Blvd, Lake Buena Vista 🌐fourseasons.com · $$$

Regular guests of the Four Seasons will know what to expect at this Floridian outpost: genuine five-star luxury. It's an indulgent resort experience, with classily understated interiors, exceptional service, and

private transfers to the theme parks. Adults-only pools and complimentary kids' clubs give everyone the space they need, while Disney character meet-and-greets promise fun for the whole family.

Lake Buena Vista Resort Village and Spa

📍G3 🏠 8113 Resort Village Drive 🌐lbvorlandoresort. com · $$

For those willing to sacrifice themed world building for a convenient homebase and budget-friendly amenities, these condo-style suites do the job. Complimentary park shuttle services also mean you're never far from the fun either.

Disney's Old Key West Resort

📍X2 🏠 1510 N. Cove Rd, Lake Buena Vista 🌐disneyworld.disney. go.com · $$

Experience the easy-going friendliness of the Florida Keys within these landscaped tropical gardens. Loved by many for the generously sized rooms and suites, the resort also has home comforts such as kitchens and separate bedrooms. There's a handy free shuttle to the parks, but a more adventurous option is the boat journey to and from Disney Springs®.

Disney's Caribbean Beach Resort

X3 ⏁ 1114 Cayman Way, Lake Buena Vista ⓦ disneyworld.disney. go.com · $$$

Disney is all about transporting you to other worlds and this place is no different. With five villages based on Aruba, Barbados, Jamaica, Martinique, and Trinidad, this superbly styled resort brings plenty of Caribbean flavor. Guests stay in brightly colored villas, surrounded by palm trees, while on-site restaurants offers dishes such as mojo pork and coconut shrimp.

Disney's Animal Kingdom® Lodge and Villas

V3 ⏁ 2901 Osceola Phwy ⓦ disneyworld. disney.go.com · $$$

Take a walk on the wild side at this high-end safari lodge. With rooms overlooking Animal Kingdom®'s grounds, don't be surprised if a giraffe stops by your window to say hello. Topping off the experience is a water park and several restaurants, which serve African delicacies.

International Drive Area

Universal's Cabana Bay Resort

T2 ⏁ 6550 Adventure Way ⓦ universal orlando.com · $$

Want the resort experience without maxing out the credit card? Book into this place, right on the doorstep of Universal's theme parks. You'll be paying less but still get to enjoy the resort experience: fun water slides, a lazy river, and an on-site American diner await.

Floridays Resort

F3 ⏁ 12562 International Drive ⓦ floridays resortorlando.com · $$

Families will love this option – and not just for its location and free shuttles to Walt Disney World® and Universal Orlando Resort™. Suites have fully equipped kitchens and the pool hosts a play area for the kids and jacuzzi tubs for the adults.

Universal's Endless Summer Resort – Surfside Inn and Suites

T2 ⏁ 7000 Universal Blvd ⓦ universalorlando. com · $$

Pretend you're beside the seaside at this homage to beach resorts of the 60s. Rooms are bright, with marine-themed decor throughout. Adding more sunshine cheer? Regularly discounted rooms and

early park admission to The Wizarding World of Magic Potter™.

Coco Key Hotel and Water Resort

T3 ⏁ 7400 International Drive ⓦ cocokeyorlando. com · $

The highlight of this great-value, family-forward resort is undoubtedly its colossal on-site water park. Had enough of the waterslides? Daytime park excursions are relatively easy, with the hotel situated in Orlando's tourist corridor.

Westgate Lakes Resort and Spa

T4 ⏁ 9500 Turkey Lake Rd ⓦ westgateresorts. com · $$

If the parks aren't enough fun, then this lakefront resort promises to fill any gaps. In addition to mini-golf, basketball, and tennis courts, there are on-site boat rentals for an afternoon of fishing and a pirate-themed water park guaranteed to delight kids. Who needs Disney anyway?

Loews Royal Pacific Resort at Universal Orlando

T2 ⏁ 6300 Hollywood Way ⓦ universalorlando. com · $$$

Theme park aficionados look no further. Not only are guests within walking (or boating) distance of Universal Orlando Resort™, this high-end hotel all offers unlimited Express Pass upgrades.

Hyatt Regency Orlando

T4 **9801 International Drive** **hyatt.com · $$$**

What makes this particular Hyatt special? It's arguably the most luxurious option on luxury-laden International Drive. Although its main appeal is to attendees of the nearby Orlando Convention Center, its amenities – a lovely spa, tennis courts, and several pools – attract leisure guests, too.

Kissimmee and Beyond

Margaritaville Resort Orlando

G1 **8000 Fins Up Circle** **margaritaville resorts.com · $$**

The resort empire of the late country music legend Jimmy Buffet is a place of pilgrimage for his legions of fans, who don Hawaiian shirts, drink fruity cocktails, and embody his genial, island-time attitude. The rooms continue the good vibes, with suites and cottages emanating a seaside chic. Check out the Salty Rim bar, serving famous concoctions inspired by the great man's songs.

Bellavida Resort

H3 **1172 Marcello Blvd** **reunionvacationhomes. com · $$$**

Live it up at this gated resort, which promises an exclusive and tranquil vacation. Private, Mediterranean-style villas come with everything you need: multiple bedrooms, private patios and pools, and fully equipped kitchens. Meanwhile, the resort itself is laced with serene walking trails, peaceful lakes, and an exclusive clubhouse. What more do you need?

Kapp and Kappy B&B

H4 **21 N. Clyde Ave** **kappandkappy. com · $**

Offering a personal touch in a sea of branded resorts, this quaint cottage is home to a quirky and intimate B&B. Hosts Tom and Christi have curated lovely rooms with individual character and foster an idyllic atmosphere – start your day chatting with the owners over breakfast and spend the evening sipping a sundowner on the wraparound porch. A rarity in Orlando.

Galleria Palms Hotel

G1 **3000 Maingate Ln** **gphkissimmee.com · $**

Want to save your extra dollars for the theme parks and souvenir shops? Book into this perfectly comfortable, no-frills hotel. It has all the basics you could want – complimentary hot breakfast, theme park shuttle services, an outdoor pool, and clean rooms – all delivered at a at very competitive price in Orlando.

Downtown Orlando

Aloft Orlando Downtown

P3 **500 S Orange Ave** **marriott.com · $**

A youthful brand catering to budget-conscious travelers, this is a great option for visitors who don't plan to spend much time in their hotel room. That's not to say that the property is sub par; the hotel has a fashionable, vibrant aesthetic with minimalist room design. An outdoor pool, bar, and gym provide basic but perfectly functional amenities.

Grand Bohemian, Autograph Collection

P3 **325 S. Orange Ave** **marriott.com · $$$**

Historic buildings with a grand hotel ambience are few and far between in Orlando, which is precisely what makes this place so special. Sip a martini in the jazz bar (the Bösendorfer Lounge) and peruse the curated art collection to feel a world away from the theme-park cacophony.

AC Hotel by Marriott Orlando Downtown

P3 **333 S. Garland Ave** **marriott.com · $$$**

This sleek high-rise has a cosmopolitan feel, with stylish bedrooms. Its amenities take it a step above the average chain hotel, too: dine at the Spanish restaurant, refuel at the coffee shop, and enjoy city views at the rooftop bar.

Embassy Suites by Hilton Orlando Downtown

🚩 P3 🏠 191 E. Pine St 🌐 hilton.com · $$

With an enviable location on the banks of scenic Lake Eola, this three-star hotel's nature views are a welcome contrast to the concrete of Downtown. Families will love the space of each suite (some of the larger rooms even have whirlpool tubs). There's a decent complimentary breakfast, an all-day café, and an outdoor pool, too.

Crowne Plaza Orlando-Downtown, an IHG Hotel

🚩 N2 🏠 304 W. Colonial Drive 🌐 ihg.com · $

It's not just the theme parks that draw visitors to Orlando: Downtown has a host of venues that hold major concerts and sporting events. This contemporary hotel is close to a few of them, and also offers a free shuttle service to other Downtown attractions. The suites come with kitchenettes and sizable living areas, with a pool and charming bistro completing the facilities.

Marriott Orlando Downtown

🚩 P2 🏠 400 W. Livingston St 🌐 marriott.com · $$

Catching an Orlando Magic game at the KIA Center or Major League

Soccer at the City Stadium? The Downtown Marriott has unmatched convenience to Orlando's stadiums and arenas, making it the perfect stay for sports lovers. Those looking for some downtime can relax with the room's flat screen TVs and 24-hour room service.

Winter Park, Maitland, and Eatonville
....

The Alfond Inn at Rollins College

🚩 L4 🏠 300 E. New England Ave, Winter Park 🌐 thealfondinn.com · $$

Every wall in this stylish boutique hotel is covered with art – and it's far from amateur. Home to the Alfond Collection of Contemporary Art (in partnership with the nearby Rollins Museum of Art), the Alfond Inn is packed with acclaimed paintings and art installations. Want to get to know the collection? Sign up for a free art tour at the hotel lobby.

SpringHill Suites by Marriott Winter Park

🚩 K3 🏠 1127 N. Orlando Ave, Winter Park 🌐 marriott.com · $$

You can't go wrong with a stay at SpringHill Suites. Staff at this modern hotel are always incredibly friendly, the rooms are clean and spacious, and the beds are super comfortable. To top it all off, the

complimentary hot breakfast is perfect fuel for a day of exploring – Lakes Killarney, Maitland, and Osceola are within easy walking distance.

Thurston House Bed and Breakfast

🚩 K3 🏠 851 Lake Ave, Maitland 🌐 thurstonhouse.com · $$

A restored Victorian B&B like Thurston House is a hidden treasure in central Florida. The rooms have evocative, rustic furnishings, with some featuring views of Lake Eulalia. Host Beverly turns out a great cooked breakfast and the rocking chairs on the wraparound porch are a tempting place to relax at sunset.

Sheraton Orlando North Hotel

🚩 J2 🏠 600 N. Lake Destiny Rd, Maitland 🌐 marriott.com · $

Business travelers flock to this large Orlando hotel (which offers numerous conference and meeting rooms), but it's equally appealing for vacationers, too. A great outdoor pool (with a hot tub) and well-equipped gym will keep you active, while the lively Irish bar is always onhand for those looking to unwind. Upgradeable options include balcony views and Club Lounge access with complimentary breakfast and evening appetizers. The stunning atrium restaurant is also a highlight.

INDEX

Page numbers in **bold** refer to main entries.

50s Prime Time Café 84, 105
1900 Park Fare 85

A

Accessibility 143
Accommodation 148–51
Adventure parks
  Fun Spot America 65, 111, 120
  Nona Adventure Park 65
  Orlando Tree Trek Adventure Park 65, 117
  Pirates Cove Adventure Golf 119, 120
Airports
  getting to/from 139
  shuttle service 89
Air travel 138
Akershus Royal Banquet Hall 85
Albin Polasek Museum and Sculpture Gardens 59, 131
Alcohol 145
Alexander Springs 70
Alligators 48
Amazing Adventures of Spider-Man, The® 38, 41
AMC® Disney Springs™ 24 103
Amelia Island 95
American Adventure pavilion (EPCOT®) 28
American Ghost Adventures 123
American Revolutionary War 9
Animal Actors on Location 36
Apollo missions 52, 55
Apollo/Saturn V Center 52
Aquatica® 71, 110–111
Armstrong, Neil 55
Arnold Palmer's Bay Hill Club & Lodge 77
Atlantic Dance Hall 81
Atlantis (space shuttle) 53
Audubon Center for Birds of Prey 133

B

Baby care 146
Ballet 61
BarCodes 83
Barnstormer 63
Bars and clubs
  International Drive Area 114
  Winter Park, Maitland, and Eatonville 134

Baseball 75
Basketball 75
Beaches 12
  Gulf Beaches 92
  Merritt Island 49
Beauty and the Beast Live on Stage 31
Behind-the-scenes tours 147
Bicycle rental/share 141
Big Thunder Mountain Railroad 23
Bill Frederick Park at Turkey Lake 66
Birdwatching
  Audubon Center for Birds of Prey 133
  Merritt Island 49
Black Point Wildlife Drive 48
Blizzard Beach 70
Blue Harmony Spa® 73
Blue Martini 80
Blues Brothers®, The 36
Blue Springs State Park 67, 70, 95
Boating 74
  Boggy Creek Airboat Rides 78, 119, 120
  Crystal River and Homosassa Springs 79
  Merritt Island 48
  St. Johns Rivership Company 79
  Winter Park Scenic Boat Tour 64, 132, 133
Bob Carr Theatre 60
Bob's Balloon Rides 120
Boggy Creek Airboat Rides 78, 119, 120
Bok Tower Gardens 92–3
Boma – Flavours of Africa 85, 105
Bonanza Golf and Gifts 120
Boneyard, The® 33
Bösendorfer Lounge 80, 82, 125, 126
Botanical Gardens (LEGOLAND®) 45
Bourne Stuntacular, The 36
Budget tips 89
Busch Gardens® 93
Bus travel 139
Buzz Lightyear's Space Ranger Spin 22

C

Café Tu Tu Tango 85, 115
Caladesi Island State Park 92
Camp Jurassic™ 40
Canada pavilion (EPCOT®) 29

Canaveral National Seashore 66
Candlelight Processional 91
Cape May Café 85
Caro-Seuss-el™ 40, 63
Car rental 140–41
Cat in the Hat™, The 39, 63
Celebration 87, 116–17, 119
Celebration Golf Club 120
Cell phones 145
Central Florida Fair 90
Central Florida Zoo and Botanical Gardens 78
Challenger (space shuttle) 55
Champions Gate 76
Charles Hosmer Morse Museum of American Art 59, 131, 133
Chef Mickey's 85
China pavilion (EPCOT®) 28
Christiansen, Ole Kirk 47
Church Street 124, 126
Cinderella Castle 25
Cinderella's Royal Table 85, 105
Citrus industry 9, 10
Citrus Tower 78
Climate 142
Clubs see Bars and clubs; Nightlife
Coastersaurus 45
Cocoa Beach 12, 94
CoCo Key Water Resort 71
Columbia (space shuttle) 55
Comedy 60
Conquistadors 8
Cosmic Quest 53
Crime 144
Crystal Palace, The 85
Crystal River 79
Cultural venues 60–61
Currency 142
Customs information 142
Cycling 74–5, 141

D

Dali, Salvador 93
Daytona 500 75
Daytona Beach 12, 94
Daytona International Speedway (LEGO®) 46
Day trips
  North and East 94–5
  South and West 92–3
DeLeon Springs State Park 70
Department stores 86–7, 102
De Santis, Ron 11
Despicable Me Minion Mayhem 34

Dezerland Park 112
Diagon Alley™, shopping in 43, 113
DINOSAUR 33
Disabled travelers 143
Discovery Cove® 70, 109
Disney & Pixar Short Film Festival 27
Disney Enchantment 24, 103
Disney's Animal Kingdom® Park 10, 11, **32–3**, 99
Disney's BoardWalk 89, 99
Disney's Grand Floridian Resort & Spa 148
Senses Spa 72
Disney's Hollywood Studios® 11, **30–31**, 101
Disney's Lake Buena Vista 76
Disney's Magnolia 77
Disney's Palm 76
Disney Springs™ 87, 88, 99
Disney, Walt 10, 11, 100
Disney Wilderness Preserve 67
District Dive 82
Diving and snorkeling, Fun2Dive 70
Downtown Orlando 13, 122–9
hotels 150–51
itinerary 125
map 122
nightlife 126
restaurants 127
sights 123–5
Dragon, The 44–5
Drive In and Dance 36
Driving 140–41
Dr. Phillips Center for the Performing Arts 61
Drugs 145
Dudley Do-Right's Ripsaw Falls® 38
Dumbo 63
DUPLO® Valley 44
Dust, The 83

E
Eatonville *see* Winter Park, Maitland, and Eatonville
Eco tours 78–9
Electrical Water Pageant 103
Electricity supply 142
Emergency numbers 144
Empire State Building (LEGO®) 46
Entertainment venues 60–61
International Drive Area 114
LGBTQ+ 82–3
live music 80–81
Walt Disney World® Resort and Lake Buena Vista 103
Enzian Theater 60–61, 132, 133

EPCOT® 10, 11, 12, **26–9**, 100
International Flower & Garden Festival 90
International Food & Wine Festival 91
World Showcase Pavilions 12, 28–9
ESPN Wide World of Sports Complex 74, 100–101
E.T. Adventure® 34, 63
European settlers 8
Expedition Everest 32–3
Experiences 12–13

F
Falcon 9 54, 55
Falcon's Fire Golf Club 120
Fantasia Gardens 100
Fantasmic! 31, 103
Farmers' markets 13, 131
Fashion stores 86–7
Fast & Furious Supercharged™ 34
Ferrari 296 GTS (LEGO®) 46
Festival of the Lion King 33
Festivals and events 90–91
Orlando International Fringe Festival 61, 90
sporting events 75
Festival of the Trees 91
Finding Nemo: The Big Blue…and Beyond! 33
Fireworks 31, 89, 99, 103
Fishing 75
Merritt Island 48
Flight of the Hippogriff™ 40, 42, 63
Flight of Passage 62
Florida
history 8–11
LEGO® 46
Florida Aquarium 93
Florida Film Festival 90
Florida Mall 87
Florida Southern College 78, 92
Flying School 45
Food and drink 13
Lakeridge Winery 78
see also Bars and clubs; Restaurants
Football 75
Ford F-150 Lightning (LEGO®) 46
Fort Christmas Historical Park 89
Four Points by Sheraton Orlando Studio City 112
Four Seasons Resort Orlando 148
Spa 72
Tranquilo Golf Club 77
France pavilion (EPCOT®) 29
Free attractions 88–9
Fun Spot America 65, 111, 120

G
Garden Grill Restaurant 85
Gateway: The Deep Space Launch Complex 52
Gay Days 90–91
Germany pavilion (EPCOT®) 28
Ghost tours 123
Glenn, John H. Jr. 55
Golden Era 9
Golf 75, 100, 112, 119, 120
courses 76–7
Gorilla Falls Exploration Trail® 33
Government advice 142
Grad Bash 91
Grand Bohemian Autograph Collection 150
Gallery 59, 89
Poseidon Spa 73
Grand Theater 10
Great LEGO® Race, The 44
Grinchmas 91
Guardians of the Galaxy: Cosmic Rewind 27

H
Halloween Horror Nights 91
Hall of Presidents 25
Hamburger Mary's 82
Hank's 83
Hard Rock Live at Universal CityWalk™ 37, 81
Harry P. Leu Gardens 66, 88, 124
Harry Potter 13
attractions 42–3
Diagon Alley™ and Hogsmeade™ shopping 113
souvenirs 15
The Wizarding World of Harry Potter™ 13, **42–3**, 109
Harry Potter and the Escape from Gringotts™ 41
Harry Potter and the Forbidden Journey™ 43
Haunted Mansion® 25
Health 144–5
Henry B. Plant Museum 93
Heroes & Legends 53
Hidden Mickeys 101
High in the Sky Seuss Trolley Train Ride!™ 40
Hiking (Merritt Island) 49
Historic Waterhouse Residence and Carpentry Shop Museum 132–3
History 8–11
Hogsmeade™, shops and stores 113
Hogwarts™ Express 43
Hollywood & Vine 85
Hollywood Bowl (LEGO®) 46

Hollywood Drive-In Golf 112
Hollywood Rip Ride Rockit® 34, 62
Holocaust Memorial Resource & Education 59
Homosassa Springs 79
Hoop-Dee-Doo 84–5
Musical Revue 103
Horseback riding 74
Hospitality industry 10, 11
Hot air balloons 13, 120
Hotels 148–51
budget tips 89
Downtown Orlando 150–51
International Drive Area 149
Kissimmee and Beyond 150
Walt Disney World® Resort and Lake Buena Vista 148–9
Winter Park, Maitland, and Eatonville 151
House of Blues® Restaurant & Bar 80, 103
Howl at the Moon 80, 114
Hubble Space Telescope 55

I

ICEBAR 112, 114
ICON Orlando 360™ 64, 112
ID 145
If I Ran the Zoo 40
iFLY Orlando 64, 112
Illumination's Villain-Con Minion Blast 35
Imagination Zone 45
IMAX – Science on a Sphere 53
IMMERSE – Creative City Project 91
Incredible Hulk Coaster® 39, 41, 62
Indiana Jones Epic Stunt Spectacular 30
Indian Removal Act 9
Indigenous peoples 8–9
Insurance 143, 145
International Dragon Boat Festival 91
International Drive Area 108–115
bars, clubs, and entertainment 114
Diagon Alley™ and Hogsmeade™ shopping 113
eye-openers on I-Drive 112
hotels 149
map 108
restaurants 115
sights 109–113
International Space Station 55
Internet access 145

Itineraries
2 Days in Orlando 14–15
4 Days in Orlando 16–17
A Day Downtown 125
A Day in Kissimmee 119
A Day in Winter Park 133
It's a Small World 25
It's Tough to Be a Bug!® 33
Ivanhoe Row 87

J

Jackson, General Andrew 9
Japan pavilion (EPCOT®) 28
Jedi Training Trials of the Temple 31
Journey into Imagination with Figment 26
Journey to Mars 53
Jungle Cruise 23
Juniper Springs 70
Jupiter C 54
Jurassic Park® Discovery Center 40
Jurassic Park River Adventure® 39
JW Marriott Grande Lakes, eco tours 78–9

K

Kali River Rapids® 33
Kang and Kodos Twirl 'n' Hurl 36
Kennedy Space Center Visitor Complex 12, 48, 52–5, 95, 118
history 10, 11
rockets: past, present, and future 54
space shuttle 55
U.S. crewed space program events 55
Kennedy Space Visitor Center (LEGO®) 46
Kilimanjaro Safaris® 32
Kings Dining & Entertainment 112
Kissimmee and Beyond 116–21
hotels 150
itinerary 119
leisure pursuits and activities 120
map 116–17
restaurants 121
sights 116–19
Knight Bus™, The 43
Kraft Azalea Gardens 89
Kraken® 63
KSC Explore Tours 53

L

Lake Apopka Wildlife Drive 67
Lake Buena Vista see Walt Disney World® Resort and Lake Buena Vista

Lake Eola Park 66, 88, 123
Lakefront Park 71, 119
Lake Lily Park 133
Lake Louisa State Park 66
Lakeridge Winery 78
Language 143
LEGOLAND® 44–7, 116
history of LEGO® 47
larger than life LEGO® creations 46
tickets 146
Water Park 45
LEGO® Movies in 4D 45
LGBTQ+
2016 nightclub attack 11
Gay Days 90–91
safety 144
venues 82–3
Lines 146
Living with the Land 27
Loews Portofino Bay Hotel
Mandara Spa 72
music at Harbor Piazza 88
Luminous: The Symphony of Us 103

M

Madame Tussauds 112
Mad Tea Party 25
Magic Carpets of Aladdin, The 63
Magic Kingdom® Park 11, 22–5, 101
Maitland see Winter Park, Maitland, and Eatonville
Maitland Art Center 59, 133
Maitland Historical Museum 133
Mako 62
Mall at Millenia 86
Manatee Observation Deck (Merritt Island) 48
Manatees 48, 70, 79
Mandara Spa at Walt Disney World Swan and Dolphin Resort 72–3
Mango's Tropical Cafe 83, 114
Manta® 62
Many Adventures of Winnie the Pooh 23
Maps
Day trips North and East 94
Day trips South and West 92
Downtown Orlando 122
Explore the Highlights 20–21
International Drive Area 108
Kissimmee and Beyond 116–17
Walt Disney World® and Lake Buena Vista 98
Winter Park, Maitland, and Eatonville 130

Marathons 75, 91
Mardi Gras 91
Medical care 144–5
MEN IN BLACK™ Alien
    Attack™ 35
Mennello Museum of
    American Art 58, 124, 125
Mercury Atlas 54
Mercury Redstone 54
Merritt Island National
    Wildlife Refuge 11, 13,
    48–9, 95, 119
    map 16
    transport 17
Me Ship, The Olive® 40
Mexico pavilion (EPCOT®) 28
Mickey & Minnie's Runaway
    Railway 30
Mickey's Not-So-Scary
    Halloween Party 91
Mickey's PhilharMagic 25
Mickey's Very Merry Christmas
    Party 91
Migrations 49
Military History, Museum of
    120
Mission: SPACE® 26
Mokara Spa at the Omni
    Orlando Resort 73
Money 142, 143
Morocco pavilion (EPCOT®) 28
Moultrie Creek, Treaty of 9
Mount Dora 95
Movies, Universal Studios
    Florida™ 37
Muppet™ Vision 3D 31
Museums and galleries 58–9
    Albin Polasek Museum and
        Sculpture Gardens 59,
        131
    Charles Hosmer Morse
        Museum of American Art
        59, 131, 133
    Grand Bohemian Gallery
        59, 89
    Henry B. Plant Museum 93
    Historic Waterhouse
        Residence and Carpentry
        Shop Museum 132–3
    Holocaust Memorial
        Resource & Education
        59
    Madame Tussauds 112
    Maitland Art Center 59,
        133
    Maitland Historical Museum
        133
    Mennello Museum of
        American Art 58, 124,
        125
    Museum of Military History
        120
    Orange County Regional
        History Center 58, 125
    Orlando Museum of Art
        (OMA) 13, 58, 123, 125

Museums and galleries (cont.)
    Orlando Science Center 13,
        58, 123, 125
    Pioneer Village at Shingle
        Creek 117, 119
    Ripley's Believe It or Not!®
        Odditorium 64, 111,
        112
    Rollins Museum of Art
        58–9, 131
    Salvador Dali Museum
        93
    Telephone Museum
        (Maitland) 59
    Titanic: The Artifact
        Exhibition 64, 109
Music 60–61
    live venues 80–81
    Musica della Notte 88
Mystic Fountain, The 40

N
Name tags 147
Napituca Massacre 8
NASA 11, 48
National parks 13
Natural springs 67, 70, 95
Nature reserves 13, 66–7
    Canaveral National
        Seashore 66
    Disney Wilderness Preserve
        67
    Merritt Island National
        Wildlife Refuge **48–9**, 95,
        119
    Tosohatchee Wildlife
        Management Area 67
New Smyrna Beach 94
Nightlife 16
    Downtown Orlando 126
    International Drive Area
        114
    Walt Disney World® Resort
        and Lake Buena Vista
        103
    Winter Park, Maitland, and
        Eatonville 134
Nighttime Lights At
    Hogwarts™ Castle 43
Nona Adventure Park 65
Norway pavilion (EPCOT®)
    28–9

O
Off the beaten path 78–9
'Ohana 85, 104
Oktoberfest 12, 28
Old Town 118
Ollivanders™ 43, 113
One Fish, Two Fish, Red Fish,
    Blue Fish™ 40
Opening hours 143
Orange County Regional
    History Center 58, 125
Orlando Ballet 61
Orlando Family Stage 60

Orlando International Fringe
    Festival 61, 90
Orlando International
    Premium Outlets 86
Orlando Museum of Art
    (OMA) 13, 58, 123, 125
Orlando Philharmonic 60
Orlando Science Center 13,
    58, 123, 125
Orlando Shakes 61
Orlando Tree Trek Adventure
    Park 65, 117
Orlando Vineland Premium
    Outlets 86
Orlando Watersports
    Complex 64
Osceola Arts 60, 120
Outdoor activities 74–5
Outta Control Magic Comedy
    Dinner Show 84

P
Pandora - The World of Avatar
    32, 103
Parent-swaps 147
Park Avenue 87, 131, 133
Parks and gardens 66–9
    Albin Polasek Museum and
        Sculpture Gardens 59,
        131
    Bill Frederick Park at Turkey
        Lake 66
    Bok Tower Gardens 92–3
    Botanical Gardens
        (LEGOLAND®) 45
    Busch Gardens® 93
    Central Florida Zoo and
        Botanical Gardens 78
    Dezerland Park 112
    Fort Christmas Historical
        Park 89
    Harry P. Leu Gardens 66, 88,
        124
    Kraft Azalea Gardens 89
    Lake Eola Park 66, 88,
        123
    Lakefront Park 71, 119
    Lake Lily Park 133
    Rocket Garden 53
    University of Central Florida
        Arboretum 88–9
    Winter Park 64, 90
    see also Adventure parks;
        National parks; Nature
        reserves; State parks;
        Theme parks
Passes 89
    theme parks 146
    Universal Express™ 35
Passports 142
Pegasus 54
Personal security 144
Peter Pan's Flight 22, 63
Pharmacies 145
Pine Island Conservation
    Area 49

Pioneer Village at Shingle Creek 117, 119
Pirates of the Caribbean® 22
Pirates Cove Adventure Golf 119, 120
Pirate's Cove Live Water Ski Show 45
Pirate Shores (LEGO®) 46
Plaza Live 81
Pointe Orlando 87
Police 144
Po Live 36
Ponce de Leon, Juan 8, 9
Popeye & Bluto's Bilge-Rat Barges 38
Population 10
Poseidon's Fury® 38–9
Postal services 145
Prices
    average daily spend 142
    public transportation 138
Prince Charming Regal Carrousel 23
Pteranodon Flyers® 38, 63
Public transportation 139
    tickets 138

R

Race Through New York Starring Jimmy Fallon 34
Raglan Road 81
Rainforest Café 84, 105
Refunds 145
Relâche Spa at the Gaylord Palms 72
Renaissance Theater Company 83
Responsible tourism 145
Restaurants 13, 84–5
    budget tips 89
    Disney and Universal characters 85
    Downtown Orlando 127
    International Drive Area 115
    Kennedy Space Center 53
    Kissimmee and Beyond 121
    theme parks 26, 30, 38, 85
    Walt Disney World® Resort and Lake Buena Vista 104–5
    Winter Park, Maitland, and Eatonville 135
Reunion Golf 77
Reunion places (theme parks) 147
Revenge of The Mummy® 34
Rides
    gentler 63
    restrictions 147
    thrill 62–3
    see also Roller coasters; Theme parks
Ripley's Believe It or Not!® Odditorium 64, 111, 112

Ritz Carlton Grande Lakes
    eco tours 78–9
    Golf Club 77
    Spa 73
Rocket Garden 53
Rocket launches 52
Rockets 54
Rock 'n' Roller Coaster® Starring Aerosmith 31, 62
Rock the Universe 91
Rodeos 75, 118
Roller coasters 13, 62–3
Rollins Museum of Art 58–9, 131
Rules of the road 138, 141

S

Safari Wilderness Ranch 78, 117
Safety
    government advice 142
    personal security 144
St. Johns Rivership Company 79
SAK Comedy Lab 60
Salvador Dali Museum 93
Saturn 1B 54
Saturn V 54
Savoy Orlando 83
Sci-Fi Dine-in Theater Restaurant 84, 105
Seas with Nemo & Friends 26
SeaWorld® Orlando 111
    controversy 111
Sebastian Inlet 94–5
Selfies, superstar 12
Seminole Wars 8–9
Seven Dwarfs Mine Train 22–3
Seven Years' War (French and Indian War) 9
Shepard, Alan B. Jr. 55
Shopping 86–7
    Diagon Alley™ and Hogsmeade™ 43, 113
    Harry Potter-themed souvenirs 15
    Walt Disney World® Resort and Lake Buena Vista 102
Shuttle Launch Experience 53
Silver Springs State Park 70
Silver Spurs Rodeo 75, 118–19
Simpsons Ride™, The 35
Skull Island: Reign of Kong 39, 41
Sky-diving 64
Sleuths Mystery Dinner Shows 84
Smaller attractions 64–5
Smoking 145
Soarin' Around the World 27
Soccer 75
Social, The 81, 125, 126
Southern Nights 82
Space Mountain® 23

Space program events, U.S. crewed 55
Spaceship Earth 27
Space shuttle 53, 55
Spas 13, 72–3
Special requirements, travelers with 143
Speed limit 138
Spell Casting – Interactive Wand Experiences 42
Splash Mountain® 62
Splash pads (EPCOT®) 71
Splitsville Luxury Lanes™ 99, 103
Sports 74–5
Star Tours® 30
State parks
    Blue Spring State Park 67, 70, 95
    Caladesi Island State Park 92
    DeLeon Springs State Park 70
    Lake Louisa State Park 66
    Silver Springs State Park 70
    Wekiwa Springs State Park 67, 70
St Augustine 95
Stetson Mansion 79
Storm Force Accelatron® 40
Street performances, Harry Potter™ 43
Stroller rental 146
Studio Audience Center (Universal) 37
Summit Plummet 63
Surfing 75

T

Tap water 144
Taxes 145
Taxis 140
Telephone Museum (Maitland) 59
Telephones 145
Tennis 74
Test Track (EPCOT®) 26
Theaters 60–61, 83
Theft 144
Theme parks
    Disney's Animal Kingdom® Park 10, 11, 32–3, 99
    Disney's Hollywood Studios® 11, 30–31, 101
    EPCOT® 10, 11, 12, 26–9, 100
    events 91
    gentler rides 63
    history 10, 11
    LEGOLAND® 44–7, 116
    Magic Kingdom® Park 11, 22–5, 101
    restaurants 26, 30, 38, 85, 105
    thrill rides 62–3
    tips 146–7

Theme parks (cont.)
transportation 141
Universal's Islands of
Adventure™ **38–41**, 109
Universal Studios Florida™
11, 13, **34–7**, 109
The Wizarding World of
Harry Potter™ 13, **42–3**,
109
Thornton Park 125
Thrill rides 62–3
Tiana's Bayou Adventure 22
Tickets
budget tips 89
public transportation 138
theme parks 146
Time zone 144
Timucua people 8
Tin Roof 81
Tipping 143
Titan Centaur 54
Titanic: The Artifact Exhibition
64, 109
Titan II 54
Tomorrowland™ Transit
Authority PeopleMover 24
Topolino's Terrace 85
Tosohatchee Wildlife
Management Area 67
Toy stores 102
Toy Story Land 30
Train travel 138–9
Tranquilo Golf Club at Four
Seasons 77
Transformers: The Ride-3D 35
Transportation
budget tips 89
getting around 138–41
theme parks 141
Travel
government advice 142
responsible tourism 145
Tree of Life Awakenings 103
T-REX® 84, 104
Trolleys 139
I-Ride 89, 110, 139
Trolls Trollercoaster 36
Turtle Talk with Crush 26–7
Tusker House Restaurant 85
TV shows 37
Twilight Zone Tower of
Terror® 31, 63
Typhoon Lagoon 70

U

Under the Sea - Journey of
the Little Mermaid 24
United Kingdom pavilion
(EPCOT®) 29
Universal CityWalk™ 87, 88
Universal Express™ 35
Universal Orlando Resort™ 11
tickets and passes 146
VIP tours 147
Universal Orlando's Horror
Makeup Show™ 36

Universal's Islands of
Adventure™ **38–41**, 109
fun facts 41
gentler attractions 40
Harry Potter attractions
42–3
"state-of-the-future" rides
41
Universal's Superstar Parade™
36
Universal Studios Florida™ 13,
34–7, 109
behind the scenes 37
Harry Potter attractions
42–3
kids' attractions 36
Universal's Volcano Bay™ 71
University of Central Florida
Arboretum 88–9
U.S. Capitol Building (LEGO®)
46

V

Vaccinations 143
¡Vamos! – Báilalo! 36
Vegas Strip (LEGO®) 46
VelociCoaster 39
Vietnamese District 124
Villas of Grand Cypress Golf
Club 76
VIP tours 147
Visas 142

W

Wagon rides 75
Waldorf Astoria
Golf Club 76
Spa 73
Walking (pedestrians) 141
Wall Street Plaza 16
Walt Disney World®
behind-the-scenes tours
147
construction/opening 10, 11
tickets and passes 146
VIP tours 147
Walt Disney World® Railroad
25
Walt Disney World® Resort
and Lake Buena Vista
98–107
hotels 148–9
map 98
nighttime attractions 103
resort area restaurants 104
shopping 102
sights 99–101
theme park restaurants
105
Water, drinking 144, 146–7
Water parks 12
Aquatica® 71, 110–111
Blizzard Beach 70
CoCo Key Water Resort 71
Discovery Cove® 70, 109
LEGOLAND® Water Park 45

Water parks (cont.)
Orlando Watersports
Complex 64
Typhoon Lagoon 70
Universal's Volcano Bay™
71
Walt Disney World® Resort
and Lake Buena Vista
101
Watersports 75
Websites 144
Wekiwa Springs State Park
67, 70
White, Edward H. Jr. 55
Wi-Fi 145
Wildlife 13
Audubon Center for Birds
of Prey 133
Central Florida Zoo and
Botanical Gardens 78
Disney's Animal Kingdom®
Park 10, 11, **32–3**, 99
Florida Aquarium 93
Lake Apopka Wildlife Dr 67
manatees 70, 79
Merritt Island 48–9
migrations 49
Safari Wilderness Ranch 78,
117
SeaWorld® Orlando 111
Zoo Tampa at Lowry Park
93
see also Nature reserves
Winter Park 64, 90
Winter Park Farmers' Market
13, 131
Winter Park, Maitland, and
Eatonville 130–35
bars and nightlife 134
hotels 151
itinerary 133
map 130
restaurants 135
sights 131–3
Winter Park Scenic Boat Tour
64, 132, 133
Winter Park Sidewalk Arts
Festival 90
Winter Summerland 100
Wizarding World of Harry
Potter™, The 13, **42–3**, 109
WonderWorks 65, 110, 112
Woody Woodpecker's
Nuthouse Coaster® 63
World Showcase Pavilions
(EPCOT®) 12, 28–9
Wright, Frank Lloyd 78, 92

X

X-15 54

Y

Ybor City/Centro Ybor 92

Z

Zoo Tampa at Lowry Park 93

ACKNOWLEDGMENTS

This edition updated by

Contributor Paul Oswell

Senior Editor Alison McGill

Senior Designers Laura O'Brien, Vinita Venugopal

Project Editors Lucy Sara-Kelly, Aimee White

Project Art Editor Ankita Sharma

Editors Ishita Chatterjee, Anjasi N.N.

Proofreader Kathryn Glendenning

Indexer Helen Peters

Picture Research Manager Virien Chopra

Senior Picture Researcher Nishwan Rasool

Assistant Picture Research Administrator Manpreet Kaur

Publishing Assistant Simona Velikova

Jacket Designer Laura O'Brien

Jacket Picture Researcher Claire Guest

Senior Cartographic Editors Subhashree Bharati, James Macdonald

Cartography Manager Suresh Kumar

Senior DTP Designer Tanveer Zaidi

DTP Designer Rohit Rojal

Pre-production Manager Balwant Singh

Image Retouching-Production Managers Pankaj Sharma, Jagtar Singh

Production Controller Kariss Ainsworth

Managing Editors Beverly Smart, Hollie Teague

Managing Art Editor Gemma Doyle

Senior Managing Art Editor Priyanka Thakur

Art Director Maxine Pedliham

Publishing Director Georgina Dee

DK would like to thank the following for their contribution to the previous editions: Richard Grula, Cynthia Tunstall, Jim Tunstall, Laura Lea Miller, Departure Lounge London.

First edition 2002

Published in Great Britain by Dorling
Kindersley Limited, DK, 20 Vauxhall Bridge Road,
London SW1V 2SA

The authorised representative in the EEA is
Dorling Kindersley Verlag GmbH. Arnulfstr.
124, 80636 Munich, Germany

Published in the United States by DK Publishing,
1745 Broadway, 20th Floor, New York, NY 10019, USA

Copyright © 2002, 2025 Dorling Kindersley Limited
A Penguin Random House Company

24 25 26 27 10 9 8 7 6 5 4 3 2 1

A CIP catalog record for this book
is available from the British Library.

A catalog record for this book is available
from the Library of Congress.

ISSN: 1479-344X
ISBN: 978 0 2416 7709 4

Printed and bound in China

www.dk.com

MIX
Paper | Supporting
responsible forestry
FSC™ C018179

This book was made with Forest
Stewardship Council™ certified
paper – one small step in DK's
commitment to a sustainable future.
Learn more at **www.dk.com/uk/
information/sustainability**